A Biological
Brain
in a
Cultural
Classroom

Robert Sylwester

A Biological Brain in a Cultural Classroom

Applying

Biological Research

to Classroom

Management

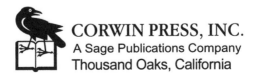

CORWIN PRESS, INC.
A Sage Publications Company
Thousand Oaks, California

For information:

Corwin Press, Inc.
A Sage Publications Company
2455 Teller Road
Thousand Oaks, California 91320
E-mail: order@corwinpress.com

Sage Publications Ltd.
6 Bonhill Street
London EC2A 4PU
United Kingdom

Sage Publications India Pvt. Ltd.
M-32 Market
Greater Kailash I
New Delhi 110 048 India

Printed in the United States of America

Library of Congress Cataloging-in-Publication Data

Sylwester, Robert.
    A biological brain in a cultural classroom : Applying biological research to classroom management / by Robert Sylwester.
        p. cm.
    Includes bibliographical references and index.
    ISBN 0-8039-6744-6 (cloth : alk. paper)
    ISBN 0-8039-6745-4 (pbk. : alk. paper)
    1. Classroom management—Psychological aspects. 2. Learning—Physiological aspects. 3. Brain. 4. Teacher-student relationships. I. Title.
    LB3011.5 .S95 2000
371.102′4—dc21   00-008092

This book is printed on acid-free paper.

00   01   02   03   04   05   06   7   6   5   4   3   2   1

Corwin Editorial Assistant: Catherine Kantor
Production Editor: Denise Santoyo
Editorial Assistant: Cindy Bear
Typesetter/Designer: Tina Hill
Cover Designer: Tracy E. Miller

Contents

Preface

M y original plan was to become a biologist, and so I focused on biology during my undergraduate years. Ecology interested me the most. My first postcollege job, however, was to teach 36 students in an eight-grade, one-room rural school. Because I also drove the bus, I was continuously with my aged 6 through 14 students from the first pickup at 7:30 a.m. to the final drop-off at 4:00 p.m. The concept of a substitute teacher (let alone of an aide or custodian) did not exist.

Overwhelmed, I came to peace with my situation by viewing it ecologically, and I became fascinated by the notion of a classroom as an ecological system of checks and balances by a focus on the logical consequences of behavior rather than on punishment. I began a graduate program during my 9 years as an elementary teacher, but I veered from biology into education (although I increasingly focused on such biologically related educational issues as learning and behaving, and on such ecological issues as space and time relationships and the distribution of power and resources in school). My doctoral dissertation focused on classroom management, a key ecological concept in education. Biological research focuses on organisms and their behavior, so I sought to discover how students view their own behavior: their view of what they do that annoys teachers, how teachers respond to such annoyances, and how fair and effective teachers are.

I discovered that even young students are keen observers of their situation. Well, why not? Their well-being during the school day depends on it. Most know more about their teachers than their teachers know about them because they only have to observe one teacher, whereas the teacher's observations are spread out among the entire class. I discovered that students consider fairness (the ecologically equitable distribution of authority, effort, and re- sources) to be a critically important component of school life.

I translated my dissertation research and management beliefs into two professional books early in my college teaching career. I continued my interest in classroom management, and regularly taught a graduate seminar on it for more than 25 years. Our under- standing of stress (and its effect on behavior and misbehavior) and of the brain systems that trigger stress and process cognition increased dramatically during this period, and so my focus on the biological and ecological substrate of educational policy and prac- tice intensified.

I also always spent a lot of time in schools working with practicum students and observing student behavior. Most student projects in my classroom management seminar gathered and ana- lyzed behavioral and opinion data from students (generally their own). These informal investigations solidified my belief that K-12 students know and feel more about classroom management issues than we often realize, and that the worst-behaved students (from the teacher's perspective) often have the most astute opinions about what is going on. K-12 students may be right or wrong, in- formed or uninformed, but it is foolish for educators to be ignorant of and/or to ignore what students believe. If for no other reason, they outnumber us.

We have always used extrinsic rewards and punishments to prop up adult control of formal education, and we currently seem obsessed with the biologically quaint notion that we can precisely measure all important forms of learning and achievement (let alone agree on what is important) in an increasingly competitive school environment. I thus thought it might be a worthy enterprise at this point in my career to revisit what I focused on first in my career, to see if the recent biological discoveries and my professional expe- riences have anything helpful to say to the current and continuing dilemma about how best to manage formal education in a demo- cratic society. That's the original impetus for this book.

In partial preparation, for the first time in decades I reread my dissertation and my first two books. I was so proud of them when I wrote them, and I am so thankful now that they are out of print. Still, the basic biological and ecological beliefs that began my professional and writing career continue to beat strongly within me: (a) Students should learn how their own biological systems function (and especially their cognitive systems), now that that knowledge and its relationship to behavior is becoming available; (b) students should participate in classroom management decisions as much as possible; and (c) it is difficult at best to separate classroom management from instruction.

In a complex democratic society, participation means that sometimes a student's views will prevail and sometimes not, but students at least ought to have an opportunity to participate in decisions that affect them if they are old enough to attend school. How else could they develop the requisite participation skills needed by citizens in a democratic society? This book will explore the key dimensions of these beliefs and suggest how educators might involve students in the search for and the direction of their own education.

I am writing this introduction on the day after Labor Day. Fifty years ago today, I drove the bus and taught my 36 students for the first time. It has been a long and satisfying trip from bus to word processor, and I have many folks to thank: (a) the research biologists who are actually doing what I originally set out to do, and who now are dramatically expanding our understanding of our brain, body, and culture; (b) the thousands of students from age 6 to more than 60 who told me much about themselves, and much about me that I had not realized; (c) the many fine editors and colleagues who helped me to find my own explanatory and interpretive voice; and (d) most important, my very loving and supportive wife, children, and grandchildren who helped me to find, live, and enjoy my own life.

Acknowledgments

The contributions of the following reviewers are gratefully acknowledged:

Ron Brandt
Editor Emeritus, Educational Leadership/ASCD
Alexandria, Virginia

Judy Hughey
Education Psychology & Counseling, Kansas State University
Manhattan, Kansas

David Scheidecker
English Department Chair, Reed-Custer High School
Bourbonnais, Illinois

Jed Schenck, PhD
Education Consulting & Cognitive Research, KNOWA
Alexandria, Virginia

Jerry Tollefson
Principal, Marquette Elementary School
Madison, Wisconsin

About the Author

Robert Sylwester is Emeritus Professor of Education at the University of Oregon. His work focuses on the educational implications of new developments in science and technology. He is the author of several books, including *Student Brains, School Issues* (1998), and *A Celebration of Neurons: An Educator's Guide to the Human Brain* (1995), and has written numerous journal articles. The Education Press Association of America gave him Distinguished Achievement Awards for his 1994 and 1995 syntheses of cognitive science research, published in *Educational Leadership*. He has made over 1,000 conference and inservice presentations on educationally significant developments in brain and stress theory and research. He can be contacted at bobsyl@uoregon.edu.

Robert Sylwester's correct e-mail address is

bobsyl@oregon.uoregon.edu

CORWIN
PRESS

The Corwin Press logo—a raven striding across an open book—
represents the happy union of courage and learning. We are a
professional-level publisher of books and journals for K–12 educators, and we are committed to creating and providing resources
that embody these qualities. Corwin's motto is "Success for All
Learners."

Chapter ❶

The Biological and Cultural Foundations of Classroom Management

●─────────────────────────●

S chools continually confront the problem of determining how to insert about 100 pounds of student brain tissue (and accompanying bodies) into a 1,000 square foot classroom, and then how to manage it appropriately during a 1,000-hour school year—biologically, ecologically, and developmentally. Because we educators attempt to enhance our students' abilities to successfully confront life's challenges, you would think that students would be pleased and appreciative of our efforts, and so would participate joyfully in all classroom activities. Think again.

Classroom management is generally a major concern of beginning teachers (and so also of their administrators), and most teachers consider it a difficult aspect of their assignment throughout their career. Our profession has consequently developed an extensive classroom management literature. Some proposed programs focus principally on institutional values such as a smoothly functioning, relatively quiet classroom, and others focus on the developmental needs and/or legal rights of students, but most attempt to create a reasonable balance between institutional and personal needs. In sum, the classroom management literature tends to view management as a teacher responsibility, and misbehavior as a problem that teachers have with students rather than the reverse. Regrettably, teacher misbehavior may well be the cause of some (if not much) disruptive student misbehavior.

To further complicate things, educators must now also consider recent developments in the biological sciences that provide intriguing new perspectives of student and teacher behavior, misbehavior, and classroom management. These developments focus on such factors as innate predispositions, the relative interactive strengths of various neural systems, normal and abnormal fluctuations in hormonal and neurotransmitter levels, and stress mechanisms and processes. Knowing that a biochemical imbalance at least partially led to the inappropriate behavior of a teacher and/or student certainly does not solve the immediate management problem, but *knowing why* generally leads to *knowing how to.* New creative and compassionate approaches to classroom management will certainly emerge over time out of this knowledge, just as they emerged in the management of mental illness once researchers and clinicians understood its biological substrate.

This book will thus focus on how our profession might begin to explore how to incorporate a biological-ecological perspective into classroom management policies and practices. It will not suggest a handful of magic procedures for getting students to behave. Rather, it will provide the functional biological background information on behavior and suggest intriguing exploratory metaphors and activities—things that you will find useful as you begin to work with colleagues and students in the observation, discussion, and informal investigation of school behaviors that will lead you to a better understanding of behavior and its management. Appropriate practical applications will certainly emerge out of such joint exploratory efforts. Some may emerge quickly, others years from now, but nothing will change if we do not begin the process.

Further, classroom management is not something totally separate from curriculum and instruction. Management issues tend to focus on behavior, but most school behavior is closely associated with curricular and instructional concerns, and there are no magic solutions to curricular and instructional issues.

Compare a cook and a chef. Both can create very nutritious and delicious food, but they differ when things go wrong in preparation. For example, a recipe-driven cook who lacks an important recipe ingredient cannot proceed without it, but a chef who understands the chemistry of ingredients and cooking processes can imaginatively substitute for the missing ingredient. Similarly, *cook-teachers* can successfully follow established management procedures, but they are limited in their ability to improvise when the procedures do not work. Conversely, *chef-teachers* understand both behavior and procedures, and so they can successfully improvise when conditions require it. This book is thus for *chef-teachers* and *apprentice chef-teachers* who want to get beyond the recipe orientation that has dominated classroom management for decades.

So as you read on, repress (at least slightly) our profession's almost innate tendency to seek immediate practical applications of new developments. Useful applications generally do not immediately emerge from major scientific developments. The DNA code was discovered in 1953, but most genetic engineering has occurred during this past decade, and cloning did not emerge until mid-1997. Furthermore, it is quite a trip from the tightly controlled variables of cognitive science laboratory research to messy classroom research, where the variables bounce off the walls.

Practical applications? What are the practical applications of an infant? It is a wet, noisy pet, at least 20 years from a clear sense of how it will turn out. What we do with infants is observe them carefully and nurture them. We try out things such as music lessons and ball-hitting if we note interest and ability, but we do not make wild promises about accomplishments (except perhaps in Christmas letters). As childhood merges into adolescence, real interests and abilities become clearer, and we then invest more heavily and decisively in practical applications.

Similarly with the brain sciences—in reality still in their infancy (but growing rapidly). It is a time to put our energy into getting acquainted with this infant that will change our professional lives—to observe, explore, and nurture. Our discoveries about our own children do not generally surprise us because we have provided them with their genes and their jeans. Similarly, many discoveries from the brain sciences do not surprise us either, because we educators have been working with a room full of brains for a long time, and although we may not understand neural networks and neurochemicals, we do know a lot about how minds and bodies function. Call it folklore knowledge if you wish, but our professional instincts have generally served us well. They thus provide us with a sense of competence in our ability to go from where we are (in our understanding of classroom behavior) to where we might be (in our understanding of the biology of behavior).

So for now, just relax with the broad concept of classroom management (difficult as it may be to relax with such an emotionally charged issue). Realize that we are in this for the long haul. Think about how current management practices emerged and how you came to your own beliefs about behavior management. Let your mind fluctuate between what happens within the natural world and what happens within the classroom environment. Note similarities and differences. Consider how you might use things you learned in one environment to enhance life in the other. Mostly though, realize that the base of our professional knowledge of behavior management is now shifting from folklore to scientific knowledge, and that the revolution is occurring on our watch.

It is occurring on our watch because (as previously suggested) so much of what we now know about the biology of our body and brain has occurred during the final decade of the 20th century, amazing as that might sound. So it is almost a matter of our profession flying blind, trying to determine what to do about scientific and related cultural developments while they are still occurring.

I firmly believe that the cooperative exploration of what to do is much more exciting for a teacher and class than being told what to do, but if you really prefer a prescriptive book that explicitly tells you how to manage your classroom, this book is not for you.

To better understand the emerging century-ending biological, cultural, and institutional revolution that is the focus of this book, it might be useful to begin with a bit of historical perspective from another educational revolution related to classroom management that occurred at the beginning of the 20th century, the adage being that those who ignore history are doomed to repeat it. It is a cultural development that might be instructive on how we might effectively proceed in guiding the next century's revolution.

Democracy and Education

In retrospect, it seems such an obvious idea. Why then did it take so long for someone to think of it, and so much longer for people to accept it and to incorporate it into our schools?

By the beginning of the 19th century, the U.S. Constitution had codified the basic principles that were to define and govern our representative democracy. It took almost 100 years for a dominant voice to suggest that the policies and procedures that schools use to instruct and manage students should demonstrate the emerging democratic principles that future voters must understand if they are to function as intelligent citizens in a democratic society. Dewey's *School and Society* was published in 1899 and *Democracy and Education* in 1916. Dewey built on the previous work of others, such as the European educators Johann Pestalozzi and Frederich Froebel, but he became this century's powerful American voice in the educational revolution.

Rereading his books, it all seems logical. Why wouldn't a fledgling democratic society demand that its public schools be laboratories for democratic behavior, tuned to the cultural needs and abilities of students? Why use the 12,000 hours that K-12 students spend in school to demonstrate the competing authoritarian societal perspective that our founders rejected in our war for independence? One would think that Dewey's ideas for participatory classroom management (or something similar to them) would have been enthusiastically embraced and instituted.

In one way they were. The Progressive Education Movement led to a wide range of enthusiastic implementation strategies (such as the Gary Plan, the Dalton Plan, and the Winnetka Plan) that were widely hailed. I was born in 1927, and so I went to school during the period when these new approaches had an opportunity to become integral to the schools. Unfortunately, my schools, along with most other schools at the time, did not function on democratic principles. Far from it. We did not even explore representative democratic values. It is not that they were bad schools, but democracy was something we studied in civics class, where we learned to write down how our total government was organized, but we did not learn how to democratically organize our small classroom community.

By the mid-century, when I entered the education profession, Progressive Education was in serious decline, severely buffeted by its critics. In 1938, when he was 79, Dewey published *Experience and Education*, a somewhat poignant title for a book in which he analyzed what went wrong with his dream to incorporate democracy into education.

To simplify a complex issue, Progressive Education tried to do too much too quickly; it did not effectively provide teachers with the knowledge they needed to incorporate the ideas, and it allowed its critics to redefine the movement and then to criticize their own definition of it. These same factors led to problems that other 20th-century educational movements experienced, such as the science/math/social science programs of the 1960s and 1970s, Values Clarification Programs, and the Free School Movement.

The interesting thing is that now, at the beginning of the 21st century, many of Dewey's curricular, instructional, and management ideas have quietly been incorporated into American schools. It has taken 100 years after the movement began, which occurred 100 years after the Constitution was in place! Why so long?

This book will argue that our profession is currently at a related transformational state. A biological science revolution has been under way for some time with, as previously indicated, a major escalation during this past decade. Furthermore, it might shortly explode with important new perspectives of what it means to be human at the cellular and systems levels. For example, scientists are currently immensely interested in the development of a comprehensive brain theory that will be of the scientific magnitude of $E = MC^2$, in that it will spark a revolution in the brain sciences at the beginning of this century that will be analogous to the revolution in the physical sciences that Einstein's relativity theories sparked at the beginning of the past century. It may profoundly alter our view of ourselves, as democracy altered our view of society.

Such a global brain theory will inevitably lead to the emergence of the 21st-century versions of such folks as Dewey, Piaget, and Skinner, individuals who will translate the biological theories into teaching, learning, and classroom management theories. And why can't you or one of your students become that person?

Educators should thus begin now to explore how best to respond to the biological science revolution. It will not go away if we just ignore it. This exploration should include the study of the errors of previous failed movements that sought to transform education, and the identification of educationally significant cognitive science developments that will play important roles in the educational theory that will emerge.

As if the biological revolution is not enough to keep our profession busy, a parallel revolution is occurring in computer technology, one which has gone through three separate revolutions in the 30 years since the silicon chip was developed: from mainframe computer to personal computer to the Internet. If you think that is the end of that revolution, dream on! Imagine the classroom management issues that computers will raise as they become more integral to classroom activity.

In *Experience and Education*, Dewey (1938) made a retrospective examination of the Progressive Education Movement, the dominant educational movement of the 20th century. Our task is to make a prospective exploration of the biological science and computer technology revolutions, which may well spark the dominant educational movement of the 21st century. It took almost 200 years for democratic values to be generally assimilated into classroom life. Let us hope that the biological science and computer technology developments begin to be generally incorporated into schools within the early years of the 21st century.

As previously suggested, the exciting thing is that this is occurring on our watch, and so today's educators get to participate in the beginning of all the revolutionary excitement, turmoil, decisions, projects, plans, failures, and successes. Or else we can sit back and let others do it. (If you work with colleagues who plan to choose the latter approach, encourage them to take early retirement and so open up their professional spot for someone who will get involved.)

One never knows how a revolution will evolve. Could Einstein have predicted the mid-century dropping of atomic bombs and the end-of-the-century video games? Atomic energy and the electronic revolution both emerged out of his theories. The Chinese word for a stress-inducing *crisis* has two characters. One means danger; the other means opportunity. Expect both within this revolution.

Three Forms of Biological Inquiry

The recent explosion of new biological knowledge was sparked by three areas of inquiry that are now combining to dig even deeper into the biology of behavior.

Genetics. Genetics focuses on the processing systems that regulate cell activity and division. Our knowledge escalated with the

1953 discovery of DNA, the biological coding system (for protein synthesis) that validated the genetic principles Darwin had proposed about 100 years earlier (Calvin, 1996). With its powerful theoretic and research base, genetics is now simply exploding with major advances in genetic engineering. Shortly after the turn of the century, scientists will complete their mapping of the entire human genome of perhaps 100,000 genes—more than 3,000 of which prescribe our brain's organization, 50% more than for any other organ in our body (Wilson, 1998).

Knowing the location and sequence of all the human genes will profoundly affect the diagnosis and treatment of various genetically related diseases, in addition to the many emotional, attentional, and learning disabilities that affect school policies and practices. These advances in gene manipulation will also carry a load of moral and ethical baggage that we will have to deal with, including issues that we cannot yet imagine.

How will we manage disruptive behaviors that emerge out of strong innate predispositions? How should today's curriculum prepare students to deal with the medical, educational, judicial, and religious issues in genetics that they will confront as (hopefully) informed citizens a decade or more from now? How many current educators have the functional understanding of DNA, genetic engineering, and the issues that surround them to create such curricula?

Imaging Technology. Imaging technology monitors the operation of various body systems. For example, the technology creates computerized representations of various brain properties such as our brain's blood flow patterns, electromagnetic fields, and chemical composition. Dramatic advances in functional magnetic resonance imaging (fMRI) technology have attracted the most recent attention. fMRI can currently rapidly image 3-mm-thick slices of brain tissue, and so create a three-dimensional image of an entire brain within 2 to 6 seconds. Because the process can be repeated immediately, scientists can observe various changes in brain activity during the period of time that a participant carries out a cognitive task, a remarkable advance in our ability to directly observe and interpret normal brain behavior. Such technologies will certainly become faster and more powerful.

Furthermore, less invasive advances in imaging technology will lead to the eventual solution of current limitations that require

the participant to lie immobile in a claustrophobic laboratory setting. These advances suggest that educational researchers could
begin to use simpler imagining technologies relatively soon. Costs
and complexity have thus far focused the use of imaging technologies on medical problems and not on the curricular, instructional,
and assessment problems that concern us (Davis, 1997; Gevins,
1997; Posner & Raichle, 1994). The 66 doctoral dissertations I have
advised during my university career gathered data through such
tools as questionnaires, observations, and literature analysis. We
did reasonably well with what we had, but it is mind-boggling to
imagine how much this next level of research capability will do to
increase our biological understanding of the educative process and
the procedures we use to manage it.

Evolutionary Psychology. Evolutionary psychology is an important (somewhat hybrid) area of scholarship that has emerged during the past quarter of a century to focus on the properties that unite
(rather than separate) the human family. *Human nature* is probably
a useful descriptive term. Insights from evolutionary psychology
have led to thoughtful explorations of why we do the things that we
do, such as to develop cooperative communities, rear our children
in a nurturing family environment throughout an extended childhood, develop technologies, and support the arts and religious
organizations. Barkow, Cosmides, and Tooby (1992) provided the initial impetus, but others have recently written thought-provoking
books on various aspects of the topic (Pinker, 1997; Ridley, 1996;
Wilson, 1998; Wright, 1994).

Evolutionary psychology will be problematic for some because
it scientifically explores areas that have previously been the sole
purview of theologians and philosophers. Evolutionary psychology looks more to our biological roots than to the powerful belief
systems that have emerged within various cultures. Educators
have been only moderately successful in dealing with curricular
conflicts over Darwinian developmental principles during the past
150 years, and the final accommodation, alas, is still down the road.
How will we work it out in a democratic spirit that seeks to con-
struct bridges rather than walls?

We thus see the recent convergence of three important interrelated fields of scholarship: one focusing on cells, one on brains, and
one on human societies. What emerges from their combined work

is the set of basic concepts that can guide our exploration of the biology of behavior. Because they will provide the context for the rest of the book, let us begin by informally examining them, constantly seeking parallels between biological life and classroom life.

Key Biological Concepts

Our body and brain are awesomely complex, but they also have an elegant simplicity about them. Thus, it is possible to begin to explore the biology of classroom management by focusing on a relatively small number of key concepts rather than on a welter of scientific facts and technical terms.

An Integrated Bodybrain Tuned to Our World. At the most fundamental biological level, we have innate capacities to function effectively within the limited natural space-time world that we inhabit. We use renewable stores of energy to move about in our search for resources and to avoid dangers. Thus, space, time, energy, movement, and range are major elements in human life and, not surprisingly, also in classroom life (as Chapters 3 through 7 explore).

Body and brain? Scientists have now moved from a former separation of body and brain to a more integrated body-brain concept. For example, our immune and endocrine gland systems were formerly (but are no longer) considered totally separate from our brain, and scientists now know that hormonal and other body systems profoundly affect our emotional life. This book will thus use the term *bodybrain* when it is difficult to separate body and brain. Recall that Dewey suggested a century ago that we should educate the whole child. Comfortable furniture and clean air thus become classroom management issues when we think of the biology of classroom management.

When we focus especially on our brain's properties, scientists now know that we have a modular plastic brain and an intellect that is dynamic and distributed. These cognitive properties pose important classroom management challenges to educational leaders who wish to tune educational policy and practice to our bodybrain's biological capabilities and limitations.

A Modular Plastic Brain. Our brain has 100 billion neurons and a trillion glial support cells that combine to carry out our brain's various processing tasks. The neurons are so highly interconnected that any neuron is only a few neurons away from any other neuron (much as any of the world's billion telephones is only a few key taps away from any other phone). A multitude of neurons is thus involved in any cognitive action. But how?

Modularity means that our brain's various processing tasks are divided among a large number of separate but interrelated neuronal systems. Each system is innately dedicated to a specific task (much as certain library shelves are assigned to a given category of books), but these dedicated neuronal systems can recruit neurons from less-dedicated surrounding areas if they need more power to process their task (much as a library's shelves can be reorganized to accommodate an expanding collection of books in a category). We can observe this developing spatial inequality in the larger amount of motor cortex space dedicated to coordinating movement in a person's dominant arm/hand as compared to the other, or in the expansion of neuronal space, devoted to left-hand digital capabilities when a right-handed person becomes a violin student (Elbert, Pantex, Weinbruch, Rockstroh, & Taub, 1995).

This ability to adapt neural systems to environmental demands is called *plasticity*, and it is obviously central to what occurs through teaching and learning. Plasticity researchers have discovered that a stimulating social environment is a major enhancing factor in the physical development of a brain (Diamond & Hopson, 1998).

How does a brain organize its more than a trillion cells for effective action? At the major systems level, our brain is composed of (a) a subcortical area (the brainstem and limbic system) whose collection of pea- to walnut-shaped nuclear structures regulate many basic brain processes that look inward to our survival, emotional, and nurturing needs, and above it (b) the large, six-layer sheet of deeply folded neural tissue called the cortex. The cortex encompasses 85% of our brain, and it processes rational logical behaviors that look outward to the time-space world we inhabit.

At the cellular level, the cortex is composed principally of hundreds of millions of highly interconnected hair-thin (100-neuron) minicolumns that extend vertically through the six cortical layers. Each minicolumn is specialized to process a very specific unit of information (such as a horizontal line or a specific tone). One hundred minicolumns combine to form a macrocolumn, which can process more complex functions related to the minicolumns it incorporates (perhaps differentiate between the cello and flute versions of a tone). About 10,000 macrocolumns (a columnar aggregate of 100 million neurons) form 1 of the 52 anatomically distinct Brodman Areas that each hemisphere contains. Brodman Areas process even more complex-related functions, many of which are currently ill understood.

Thus, discrete columnar brain areas and systems process basic limited cognitive functions. These are incorporated into larger, specialized, widely distributed but highly interconnected areas and systems that collaborate on complex cognitive tasks. For example, our visual system has about 30 separate columnar subsystems that process such visual properties as shape, depth, color, quantity, and movement. Thus, the subsystem that responds to the color red processes it on every red object we see, and the subsystem that responds to circular shapes processes balls, CDs, tires, donuts, and so forth. Several of these subsystems will combine to process a single red ball rolling across a table.

This modular system of brain organization means that recent dramatic advances in brain imaging technology can help scientists identify highly specific brain areas that do not function properly in children with a specific cognitive handicap. Locating such a neurological deficit is the first step in solving the problem.

The Fast For Word (1997) program developed by the Scientific Learning Corporation emerged out of research discoveries of specific aural processing deficits in children who were seriously delayed in learning to speak and to comprehend speech. The Fast For Word program has achieved remarkable results through its use of stimulating video game technology that speeds up the child's aural processing ability. This may well be the technological prototype for future interventions that require extensive practice in order to speed up, slow down, and/or rewire the various adaptable neural systems involved in a disability. Because students who master language skills with difficulty often (understandably) create classroom behavior problems, such interventions may lead to a major reduction in some kinds of classroom management problems.

Our profession has become interested in theories of multiple intelligences in recent years, and these theories are based on our brain's modular organization. The fact that the location of most neural systems, subsystems, and interconnections involved in various intelligence categories have yet to be precisely identified does not diminish the reality of brain modularity as the biological substrate of the theories. Modularity is an important concept for educators who accept any theory of multiple intelligences, and imaging technology will shortly provide the brain map that lays out the organization of our brain's multiplicity.

This suggests that it is also important to think beyond multiplicity in intelligence. Most bodybrain systems are multiple. We obviously have multiple sensory/motor systems, and we now know that we have multiple emotional and attentional systems. We have known for some time that we have multiple memory and problem-solving systems. What we have is a multiple-everything body-brain, and intelligence is only one part of the quite intricate equation. Chapter 3 further explores this concept.

Thinking about brain modularity sparks thoughts of the analogous modular organization and management of a classroom: some 30 separate but highly integrated student systems who function separately, in parallel operations, and in competitive and cooperative modes. Cooperatively combining their capabilities generally leads to a better solution of an intrigung problem than the sum of individual solutions, so a class is sort of a social brain.

Dynamic Intelligence. We are used to thinking of intelligence as something that occurs entirely inside our brain, but this is now seen as a very narrow view of a complex process that also involves our body and the environment in which our bodybrain functions. *Dynamic* is a better term, one that combines the interactions of the three (Clark, 1998).

Candace Pert, who achieved scientific fame with her endorphin-related discoveries a quarter of a century ago, suggests in *The Molecules of Emotion: Why You Feel the Way You Feel* (1997) that biology no longer supports the notion of a body-brain separation. Hormonal peptides course throughout our bodybrain to process the emotions that drive our behavior. We are not centered in our brain but in our completely combined bodybrain. Consider the negative effects of an upset stomach on test taking if you think that intelligent behavior is all in our head.

Furthermore, we actually tend to off-load a lot of our decision making, creating external procedures and technologies that adjust energy, time, space, and movement in our environmental range to simplify intelligent decisions. For example, consider how much cognitive energy we typically spend in trying to determine which supermarket checkout stand will move the fastest, as compared to the lack of any such thought in a post office or bank with a next-available-clerk system. Imagine if a teacher had to decide how to do it every time the class went to the library or cafeteria. Established procedures and rules are integral to classroom life.

Consider the shape of a pair of scissors, and how we have created a marvelous technological extension of our hand-finger system that allows us to easily carry out a precise cutting function that would be impossible to do with our fingernails.

We use icons to simplify decisions in complex environments, an extension of the natural clues our ancestors followed to locate water and food. When driving along a succession of gaudy strip malls, easily visible corporate icons help us decide when and where to turn off for gas, food, lodging, and so forth (and to ignore all other icons that contain information we do not currently need).

Calculators and Post-it™ notes extend our limited short-term memory capacity, and telephone books and dictionaries save long-term memory energy. The list goes on and on. We have created technological capabilities on the outside of our skull to extend our inside biological capabilities, and so we cannot measure internal intelligence without factoring in the effects of the external technologies we use. Consider the foot-dragging that occurred in allowing students to use calculators in math tests, as if doing it with paper and pencil was somehow more intellectual (and did ancient educators similarly decry the intellectual loss of finger counting when paper and pencils arrived?).

The recent explosion in electronic and computer technology has moved our dynamic brain-body-environment relationship to a new level. *Natural* time, space, and energy have become *cyber* time, space, and energy, and they have escalated our ability to rapidly organize and process vast amounts of information. One dilemma is that children tend to have a better understanding of the new electronic technologies than do their parents and teachers. They have spent countless hours playing with them to explore all their possibilities, whereas we adults tend to master them only as limited tools (as an expensive typewriter, a means of keeping accounts).

Today's parents and teachers are thus often at a disadvantage when trying to help their children understand the opportunities and dangers that electronic media pose. Our 15 grandchildren are all connected by e-mail, which is a marvelous opportunity, but this capability also means that they can individually engage in chatline conversations with dangerous unseen predators.

The school must confront the dynamic nature and processes of technology, and especially electronic technology, but we seem to be moving very slowly. We are the last pencil-driven institution in our society.

I have long felt that the slow movement of multiple computers into the classroom was more related to classroom management than finances. Educators could not figure out what to do with a big box-like monitor on each student desk (let alone electrical cords everywhere). Teachers are used to seeing the top half of their student's bodies out in the open and not hiding behind monitors. The emergence of relatively inexpensive, powerful, portable, net-worked laptop computers that resemble an unobtrusive notebook binder on top of a desk suggest that a computer at every desk (with all its attendant management problems) is something that could occur relatively soon.

(Humans seem to enjoy Savannah environments: low grassy vegetation with a scattering of trees, as in parks and suburban yards. In some ways, a traditional classroom resembles a Savannah: the complex of desktops being the low vegetation, and the students a scattering of trees.)

Distributed Intelligence. Our upright stance and consequent necessarily narrow female birth canal have led to a brain that is born only one third its adult size (when compared with those of most animals that are born with an almost fully developed brain). The biological solution to the problem is to be born with a full complement of neurons, but with most neural systems functioning at only a survival level. These protosystems then mature by expanding their connections as environmental challenges dictate (and this explains the nature of the postbirth size increase). Thus an infant can innately suckle and cry, but must later learn to use its mouth and voice to sing Bach arias. The startle reflex (fear) is innate, but the child must explicitly learn how to cross a busy intersection.

We need a long childhood and explicit instruction to expand the power of our complex of neural protosystems so they can function at the sophisticated level our culture requires. This requires some kind of extended bonding between parents and between parents and children (and oxytocin, vassopressin, and endorphin seem to play important neurochemical roles in this process). Add kinship extensions, and children grow up in a dependent society. Someone will care for them during their first two decades, but then the social contract is that they will spend the next several decades caring for their children (and the children of others in our complex society).

So we are of necessity a social species. This innate sense of dependence means that everyone in a social group must be able to do some communal things (such as being able to speak the common language), but not everyone has to be able to do everything (such as being able to repair a car). Repairing a car requires specialized knowledge and skills that require extensive training, but we do not often need to repair our car. Thus, it is to everyone's advantage for a few people to specialize in car repair and maintain their abilities by doing it as a vocation, and others to specialize in something else. It is a complex tit-for-tat negotiating arrangement (you repair my car, and I will teach your children) and an extension of the concept of a dynamic brain that provides our species with an additional powerful social brain. It is simply another reason to encourage school activities that develop cooperative skills and attitudes.

School assessment programs have focused on individual student capabilities and limitations, and it is good to help students discover how their interests and abilities can be channeled into an appropriate useful vocational specialization. The seeming need for precision in assessment led to a focus on factual-computational knowledge that can be easily and precisely assessed at the cost of ignoring subjective knowledge (as in the arts and humanities) that is more difficult to precisely assess. So I look in vain for reports on the arts and humanities scores when the newspapers report the results of local school testing programs. Are 26 letters and 10 digits and name/date/place information all that our brains are about?

Goleman's (1995) excellent synthesis of the dramatic advances in emotion research alerted many educators to the terrible error we have made: to use assessment precision as a principal criterion for determining curricular importance. We have ignored the important role that emotionally driven subjective thought and curricula play in intellect. Is it really possible to remove the arts and humanities as a factor in developing intelligence?

The marvelous thing about our integrated bodybrain (our modular plastic brain and its dynamic distributed intellect) is that its definitive properties include a wide array of capabilities that emerged over eons to respond successfully to dangers and opportunities, but also to create a qualitative social life that involves loyalties, the arts, science and the humanities, belief systems, and the ability to enjoy a beautiful sunset. We do disservice to our bodybrain when we provide it with limited opportunities during its formative years. If our students can do something, they ought to have an opportunity to learn to do it properly and effectively. That is the challenge our profession confronts as we now discover our bodybrain as we never could before.

Cells and Classrooms

Life is an elusive concept, except that it exists in time and space and requires energy. The current continuing cultural controversy over abortion and euthanasia suggests that we have trouble identifying life's timing: its beginning and ending. We also have trouble locating it in space. Is life a property of the entire organism, or does it reside within individual organs, tissues, cells, or complex molecules such as DNA? We have further problems with its energy source. Is life's energy nothing more than the activity of self-organizing biological systems, or does it involve such disembodied concepts as mind, spirit, soul, or god? Is life something that exists or doesn't, such as an on/off switch, or is it emergent, like a dimming switch (and if so, what is its range)?

Three properties that are common (at several different levels) to all living organisms are (a) a semipermeable membrane covering, (b) a storehouse of unorganized nutrient materials, and (c) an organizing agent. Whether this combination of properties is actually the essence of life is an issue beyond this discussion, but these properties are important to living organisms, so let us muse about them within the context of the management of a cell and a body and a classroom.

In this metaphoric exploration, and in those to follow, I may muse on well after you have made the connection, or stretch the metaphor beyond what you would prefer. Please indulge me in this because I am trying to provide a broad metaphoric base that teachers can use with a variety of students (and thank you for your indulgence).

Semipermeable Membrane

A cell and a body exist in space and so their covering defines their location. In cells, the covering is called a semipermeable membrane, and in a human bodybrain it is the 6-pound, 20-square foot, 2-layer mantle of skin that covers our body to keep our insides in place, hold heat in, and keep infection out.

Cells and bodies interact with their outside environment, so they need mechanisms that know what to admit and exclude and that can process the in-and-out movement of materials. In a cell, these processes are carried out by receptors on the membrane that recognize various materials, and channels through the membrane that processes their in/out movement. In our body, our sensory system recognizes friends and foes, and our 30-foot long digestive tube and genital system are the principal conduits for the in/out movement of organic materials. What about the recognition of such things as love and hate, and the in/out movement of energy to process and express them? Does behavior become the avenue for sending out such messages that seem to transcend mere organic material?

The semipermeable membrane is thus an important concept in biological systems because it is about what to let in and what to exclude. So it is about food and drink, beautiful music, rape, the smell of flowers, cigarette smoke, conversation, profane and obscene comments, and a whole lot of other things. It is also about the internal products that leave our body such as urine, semen, babies, and nursing milk, but also poems, condolences, inventions, and imaginative lessons.

A classroom also has a semipermeable membrane around it. The walls, ceiling, and floor provide the basic separation from the rest of the community, and the doors, windows, electrical outlets, and faucets allow the in/out flow of students and information. They bring in televised messages from distant places and speakers from the neighborhood, children from functional and dysfunctional families, library books, and show-and-tell artifacts. By extension, a semipermeable membrane is also about a school's admission policies, classroom rules, drug policies, dress code, and hiring practices. At its core, much of classroom management is really about the concept of a semipermeable membrane. Chapter 7 explores this concept.

Unorganized Nutrient Material

The constant availability of food is a problematic issue for living organisms, so when it is available they must take in and store more than they immediately need. In a cell, this is the nutrient part of the cytoplasm that is immediately available for the assembly of such cellular products as proteins, whenever the need arises. In our body, it includes the fat layers and nutrients that circulate in our blood stream before they are taken up by cells. In our brain, it includes basic memory units and problem-solving strategies that we can combine to solve novel problems when we confront them.

Think conceptually of the difference between potential and kinetic energy. Potential energy is the stored energy available in a stationary rock poised at the top of a hill, and kinetic energy is what is expressed when the rock rolls down the hill.

Much of our body's weight is composed of currently unused fluids that slosh around waiting to get organized into something that becomes a body part or behavioral (kinetic) energy. Stored things that are not currently in use are thus important to biological survival, and we typically have a lot of potential energy within us. How much should be stored can become a biological issue, however, whether it is excess fat on our body, excess sugar or salt stored within our system, or excess drugs taken into our brain. The same issue can occur with excess arcane curricular information that took a lot of energy to get into our brain, but that has a very limited chance of ever turning into useful cognitive kinetic energy.

One can cynically think of a classroom as a collection of the unwashed and illiterate, milling aimlessly about while waiting for its Representative of Adult Civilization to organize things, and if the truth be known, students spend a lot of time waiting for something significant to occur in classrooms in which the teacher makes all the decisions. Students wait to use classroom equipment, to get their teacher's help or assurance that work is correct, to answer the teacher's question, and to leave the room. The sixth graders in a study conducted by Lyons (1977) averaged the initiation of a waiting period every 8 minutes, and generally they were waiting for their teacher's attention.

All shelved curriculum and library materials are potential energy, awaiting a kinetic opportunity to move from the shelf into a student's mind. Athletes on the sidelines are potential energy, desperately hoping to get kinetic. Potential and kinetic energy are thus important classroom management concepts, and Chapter 3 further discusses them.

Organizing Agent

Cells and organisms need a simple efficient agent to organize their nutrient materials into the products and processes that help to define life. In a cell, DNA in the nucleus and RNA (ribonucleic acid) carry out that function. Think of a cell as a kitchen, DNA as the genetic cookbook that contains recipes for all the proteins that a body can make, and RNA as the cook who reads the DNA recipe for a protein and then assembles it from the materials within the cellular cytoplasm. Just as a cook does not generally use all the recipes in a cookbook, so each cell assembles only a very limited number of proteins from the vast repertoire in our body's DNA.

All proteins are made from 20 different amino acids that can be arranged in countless sequences and lengths, just as all 500,000 English words are made from only 26 different letters that can be arranged in a great variety of sequences and lengths. The information in both proteins and words is not coded into the amino acids and letters themselves, but rather into the sequence of amino acids and letters and the length of the chain (e.g., go, god, dog, good, goods, etc.). Consider also the infinite number of melodies constructed from sequences of 12 tones, and our immense number system constructed from sequences of only 10 digits.

At the body level, our brain has the assignment of initially receiving meaningless sensory information and organizing it into an integrated coherent model of what is occurring outside our body's semipermeable membrane and then responding appropriately. Our brain also uses a functionally simple system: several dozen different kinds of neurotransmitters that move between synaptically connected neurons that function through only two response modes (excitatory and inhibitory).

Something appears to have been added at this level of organization and direction. Cellular protein production is directed by DNA-RNA-cytoplasm interactions, but their simple chemical transformations do not appear to have anything approaching the conscious purposeful cognitive activity that we sense in directing many of the activities in our brain. New elements are seemingly added as simple systems become more complex.

When we metaphorically move to the classroom level, we tend to think of the teacher, administration, or the curriculum as being the organizing agent. As with the organizing agents in our cells and bodies, the classroom organizing agent functions through a relatively simple sequential production system: a selection of activities, a schedule that sequences them, a determination of importance that decides how long activities will last (from a short, discrete lesson to an extended, integrated instructional unit), and a grouping system that ranges from individual students to various groups of students. Chapters 4 and 5 further discuss this issue.

A semipermeable membrane, an extensive collection of potentially but currently unorganized materials, and an organizing agent. Throughout history, it has been a good organizational plan for biological systems at all levels, and that includes classrooms.

Chapter ❷

The Multiple-Everything Modular Bodybrain That Schools Seek to Manage

●━━━━━━━━━━━━━━━━━━━●

C hapter 1 introduced the important concept of biological modularity—that specific bodybrain systems evolved to execute specific tasks. For example, feet walk and ears capture sounds, but many important biological tasks require complex, widely distributed systems that broadly disseminate materials and/or information. For example, our circulatory system moves a large assortment of life-sustaining molecules and blood cells that our heart pumps through a tubular bodybrain-encompassing artery/vein/capillary system that is supported by various maintenance organs (such as the kidneys and lungs). So, to simplify a complex process, the veins input blood, the heart pumps it, and the arteries output it.

At the other end of the size scale we discover that each of our 100 billion neurons is similarly an input/process/output system. A neuron's dendrites receive molecular information from other neurons, the cell body processes it, and the axon sends the molecular response on to other neurons.

Sort of resembles a school system, doesn't it, with its student admissions input, organizational/curricular/instructional/management processes, and graduation output, with a variety of central office and building subsystems to support and maintain functions?

The management of a classroom full of behaving and misbehaving students and/or teacher must begin, then, with at least a functional understanding of the key biological systems and subsystems that regulate the behavior of each individual and of the entire class group. This chapter functionally describes our principal biological systems and subsystems, and subsequent chapters explore how we can use such biological principles and systems to enhance classroom management policies and practices.

The Principal Brain Systems

Chapter 1 indicated that our brain's 100 billion neurons are initially organized into hundreds of millions of cortical columns and subcortical nuclei, which are further organized into more than 100 larger integrated processing systems—with many currently ill-understood. However, if we functionally explore our brain and its processes, we discover that it has specific complex systems that become aware of and respond to internal and external challenges (input/process/output) and that the process generally follows a rapid logical biological sequence—a sequence with intriguing parallels to the typical design and management of classroom instruction.

Important internal and external sensory information activates our arousal/alerting system (emotion), which activates our focusing system (attention), which activates our various solution systems (learning/memory, reason/logic, problem solving), which activate our response systems (behavior, movement). We thus cognitively engage, solve, and act (input/process/output). Each of these three major functions is processed by specific dedicated brain systems and subsystems: our multiple-everything brain.

As suggested earlier, our brain is awesomely complex biologically, but elegantly simple functionally. Because even primary grade students can understand its functional components, what follows is useful background information that you can use to introduce your students to their brain. Do it!

Engage

All cognitive activity is dependent on the initial activation of our integrated sensory/emotional/attentional system. It is biologically impossible to learn something if we are not attending to it, and we do not attend to things that are not emotionally meaningful to us. Educators have always intuitively known this, and yet some teachers continue to speed through this key initial process with a single dreary directive (e.g., "Clear your desk, take out your math book, and work the problems on page 23").

Because the brain sciences are now discovering how this important integrated activation system functions, we should seek to understand and emphasize it (and Chapter 3 further explores the management implications of this concept). Truly engaged students will actually do much of their exploring and learning during nonschool time, thus expanding the curriculum. We see this in childhood hobbies. Emotionally engaged children spend countless attentive hours of independent reflective time pursuing their new interest.

Senses

Our sensory system is our initial source of information on what is happening inside and outside our body's 20-square foot mantle of skin. It is composed of a complex set of specialized receptors embedded in our skin that monitor relatively narrow ranges of properties of the internal and surrounding environment. They respond especially to high-contrast changes in the composition and movement of molecules and light rays that strike our body (such as changes in temperature, air and physical pressure, reflected light rays, and the chemical composition of air, water, and food). The human visual and auditory systems are dominant, but all systems play key initial roles in our brain's task of creating perceptual meaning out of abstract sensory information.

Recent educational thought has strongly and appropriately encouraged educators to emphasize activities that engage and develop all elements of our sensory system.

Emotion

Emotion is a general term for a complex, critically important, three-part, thermostat-like arousal system that unconsciously interprets and evaluates sensory information, thus alerting us to current and potential dangers and opportunities that reach our emotional threshold. Temperament and mood can strongly affect our emotional arousal.

Temperament. Temperament provides us with a (perhaps innate) lifelong initial emotional response bias to environmental challenges. A person's temperament typically centers somewhere along a continuum between bold/uninhibited and anxious/inhibited (Kagan, 1994), with boldness processed principally in the left hemisphere, and anxiousness in the right hemisphere (Siegal, 1999).

Temperament is a useful human trait in that it allows us to quickly and confidently take the first step in response. The bold tend to go forward in curiosity (sensing an opportunity); the anxious tend to go backward in hesitant concern (sensing danger). Because we frequently follow our developing temperamental bias, we tend to become quite competent with it over time. For example, bold people tend to become skilled at responding boldly (similar to handedness, which develops exceptional competence with the favored hand).

It is important for students to realize that it is okay to generally operate out of either end of the temperament continuum. Our society profits from the strengths of those who are typically either cautious or bold (such as investors who specialize in either conservative or risky investments). Indeed, opposite temperaments often marry each other, and the relationship generally profits from the strengths of each (if they both respect their partner's temperament) because life confronts us with both dangers and opportunities. School groups often exhibit a similar temperament range, from staff and students who are stimulated by any novel idea to those who feel threatened by any change.

One classroom problem, however, is that bold/uninhibited students tend to dominate classroom life (whereas the anxious raise their hand and await their turn). Anxious/inhibited students may thus develop a sense of inferiority by incorrectly equating boldness with success. The aphorism "Fools rush in where angels fear to tread" speaks to the value of caution, but anxious/inhibited students wistfully note the attention the bold/uninhibited tend to get.

Thus it is important that we create a school atmosphere that encourages students (and especially those at the anxious/inhibited end of the continuum) to understand and accept themselves for who they are, and to positively develop their temperamental bias, but also to explore opportunities to widen their temperamental response range in appropriate situations. For example, cooperative group activities help students at both ends of the continuum to discover that the entire group can profit from temperamental diversity, and participants can assume group roles that challenge their temperamental bias.

Mood. Mood provides us with a useful short-term (hours to days) emotional response bias that we layer on to our temperament. Mood shifts probably emerge out of fluctuations in the various chemical rhythms and cycles that regulate bodybrain energy levels and functions. Mood thus informs us of our current and perhaps unconscious level of interest in the challenge, and of the amount of response energy that we currently have. We may ignore behaviors on one day that would anger us on another. Our fluctuating level of wakefulness and hunger can similarly affect our desire and ability to respond.

It is important that we communicate our current mood to others because they may then temper the demands that they make on us, effectively enhancing our ability to respond appropriately to current dangers and opportunities; and we actually do effectively communicate mood through several poorly understood forms of body language. For example, a friend suggests "I can see the anger in your eyes." Although one would be hard-pressed to state how a set of eyes can communicate such different moods as anger, joy, despair, and excitement, they seem to do it. We do tend to sense the moods of others and adapt to them if possible.

Students come to school with a wide range of moods. Because mood significantly determines response, we might begin the day with interactive activities that provide a sense of how the various moods of students might affect their behavior. We might then further adapt instruction to the moods of the participants. Teachers commonly use a variety of techniques (such as holiday decorations and activities) to stimulate similar moods in students, and so simplify classroom management and instruction.

Emotion. Emotion itself (as we typically view it) is the most immediate and volatile of the three systems that regulate arousal. Layered on to temperament and mood, it is regulated by a collection of unconscious neuronal systems that continually provide a variety of immediate, often high-energy, positive-to-negative response biases to various challenges. We often publicly communicate the nature of our emotional state through mood-enhanced body language (such as with smiles or tears). When emotion reaches our level of consciousness, it becomes a feeling—a much more private experience in that no one can truly know how we feel, even though we may talk about it.

Until recently, it was very difficult to study the specific bodybrain systems that regulate emotion, but the field is now rapidly expanding and we can expect further developments and a better understanding. It is currently not clear how to classify our various emotions (just as it has been difficult to classify the kinds of intelligence). One way to classify emotions would be to group them temporally and topically: those that respond to events that have already occurred (such as surprise, the acceptance-disgust-anger continuum, and the joy-sadness continuum), and those that prepare us to respond to events that are about to occur (such as anticipation and fear). Furthermore, the simultaneous activation of two or more of these primary emotions results in a blended emotion (such as surprise/fear = alarm, or anticipation/fear = anxiety—often a dysfunctional blended emotion because it focuses our emotional system entirely on what might occur while ignoring what is occurring). Some emotional states (such as guilt, embarrassment, pride, and jealousy) seem triggered by social events. Researchers currently best understand the neural systems that process fear and joy (or pleasure).

It is important to realize that emotions (like temperament) are neither positive nor negative in themselves. The mechanisms for each emotion evolved to bias and enhance our response to a specific type of immediate problem. The point is to avoid having such a low-firing threshold for one emotion (such as fear) that it dominates all emotional responses, or to activate an inappropriate emotion (something that occurs when people cry during weddings and laugh during funerals). Developing emotional competence is thus important in all educative activities.

Goleman's (1995) *Emotional Intelligence: Why It Can Matter More Than I.Q.* introduced many educators to the important role that emotion plays in cognition. Goleman (and now others) argues persuasively that educational activities can enhance the development and maintenance of our overall emotional system (defined here as encompassing temperament, mood, and emotion) so that it alerts us appropriately to dangers and opportunities. Young people need to create a functional balance between unconscious emotional arousal and conscious rational response that capitalizes on the role of each. Studies of people who have created such a positive balance in their lives have led to the identification of the several elements discussed below that are critical to the personal/people skills that lead to emotional intelligence, and so it is important to incorporate them into classroom life.

Intrinsic motivation. Intrinsic motivation is the self-starter's ability to persist in frustrating situations. This ability emerges out of an environment that encourages the discovery and exploration of personal interests and abilities. Such experiences create our self-concept (how we define ourselves) and our level of self-esteem (how we value that definition). Continuous informal evaluations that focus more on what we can do than on what we cannot do create a necessary climate of positive social feedback. Helpful activities are those that value and discuss feelings, that encourage multiple and cooperative approaches to problem solving, and that encourage self-assessment.

Impulse control. Impulse control is the ability to delay decision and gratification. Regrets and apologies are a part of human life, and prisons are full of people who wish that they had counted to 10 before acting. Our wary emotional brain often reads immediacy into situations that do not require immediate arousal and response and that are better solved through delayed reflective thought. Developing a pattern of assertive (rather than aggressive) responses to difficult situations enhances impulse control. Helpful activities are those that develop problem-solving skills and those that focus on long-term projects with intermediate goals (so participants can experience and appreciate things that develop slowly).

Mood regulation. Mood regulation is the ability to regulate moods (especially those related to anger), so that distress does not reduce our ability to think and to reflect. There is a fine line between simply experiencing mood for what it is and allowing it to dominate all our behavior. Although we may occasionally (and perhaps unfortunately) step over that fine line, it is probably worse to be so controlled emotionally as to never step over it. Helpful activities are those that teach students to understand and respect emotional arousal without necessarily submitting to it, and those that provide a forum for venting positive and negative emotion and an opportunity to retreat from social interaction when emotion overwhelms.

Empathy. Empathy is the ability to empathize with a sharing, caring, and hopeful sense of how the other person feels about something. Sympathy differs from empathy in that it is a kind-hearted recognition of the plight of another without the sense of sharing it that empathy implies. Empathy is an important social trait in that it leads to ethical and altruistic behaviors. Helpful activities are those that encourage constant open discussion of how things are going in order to help students tune into each other (to develop useful listening/looking/responding skills in conversation).

Social competence. Social competence is the ability to quickly size up and appropriately respond to social situations. Our complex social structure functions via our innate sense of cooperation, early experiences with adults and children, and a set of social rules (or manners) that might actually be quite arbitrary and culture driven. Manners, thus, do not come naturally but must be taught. Helpful activities are those that encourage the constant informal interactions that allow participants to discover how others respond to their behavior and that specifically teach the social conventions a group must observe if they are to effectively work together. Activities such as cooperative learning projects, games, field trips, and reflective discussions do this.

Attention

Emotional arousal is an indication that something important has occurred or is about to occur. But where? To find out, our emotions

activate attention, a complex cognitive system that selects and temporarily focuses on key emotionally important elements in an often
confusing environment and maintains goal-directed behavior in
highly distractible situations. Our attention system is composed of
a number of distinct neural networks, each of which actively carries
out specific attentional functions by itself, or in interaction with
other cognitive systems. Because experience and educational interventions can improve the efficiency of this complex system, we
should design school activities that enhance the development of
the three separate functional systems that regulate attention.

The Orienting System. The Orienting System disengages us from
what we were attending to and focuses us on the new target. We
generally shift our attention to emotionally arousing things that
contrast sharply with our current focus and ignore (or merely monitor) steady states, subtle differences, and gradual changes. For
example, when we leave a building, we consciously notice the temperature when it is much different outside than inside but not when
both are similar. We (and especially students) use the term *boring* to
describe a steady-state environment with few emotionally stimulating challenges.

Our environment, however, is replete with serious dangers
(such as pollution) that are subtle and gradual. They are emotionally significant, but we tend to focus on them only when a high contrast catastrophe (such as a toxic spill) occurs. The news is about the
unusual, not the normal, so it reports a single freeway pile-up of 10
cars but not the perhaps 100 individual fender-benders that occurred in the same general area that day. Graphs and time-lapse
photography are examples of the many technologies we have developed to observe changes that occur too gradually to activate our
biological emotion and attention systems. Many children's games
(from Simon Says to videogames) require participants to identify
and attend to important subtle clues, so children do tend to enjoy
the challenge of subtlety.

An important element in successful classroom management is
the ability to note and orient to subtle changes in students that
might lead to behavioral disruptions. During my first year of teaching, I expended much energy on classroom management problems
and was generally unsuccessful. Several years later, I spent far less

energy on management and had fewer problems. I now realize that much of the difference emerged out of experiences that taught me to attend to potential problems before they became real problems. In effect, I moved from being a few steps behind my class to being a couple steps in front of them.

The Executive Attention System. The Executive Attention System draws heavily on memory to recognize the identity of the new target (foreground), determine its significance, and separate it from the background information (which it then merely monitors or ignores). This is typically an efficient unconscious process that draws on established responses, but we do confront situations in which it is not obvious what we should focus on in a confusing situation, and so our Executive Attention System must consciously make the decision such as to respond to a novel situation that will require planning and decision making, to alter a habitual response, or to correct an error. The broad appeal of magicians and mystery stories suggests that we are stimulated by this conscious element of attention.

Our working (or short-term) memory is an important part of this system. It is a fragile, limited-capacity buffer that allows us to briefly attend to and hold a few units of information while we use it (dial the phone number) or determine its importance (the name of a stranger in a party conversation). It is about things that are important right now, but not so important that we want to remember them for the rest of our lives. The limited capacity of working memory is useful because it forces us to combine related bits of information into larger units by identifying similarities, differences, and patterns that can simplify and consolidate an otherwise large and confusing sensory field. Vocabulary categories emerged out of this cognitive ability.

Students need many opportunities to develop this important system. We should incorporate many options that require participants to make choices that they can later reflect on to determine the wisdom of their choice. Furthermore, working memory is enhanced by activities that require participants to rapidly classify large numbers of items into a smaller number of categories. Discussions and debates similarly require participants to consciously select and attend to limited information for a limited time.

The Vigilance System. The Vigilance System has the reverse task of the Orienting System. Vigilance maintains a sustained focus on something while ignoring small, random, potentially distracting environmental changes. The Vigilance System thus helps us ignore minor but not major distractions. Major distractions may lead to an emotional arousal that activates our orienting system, and we are off to a new focus of attention. We typically can simultaneously attend to several noncompeting events (such as to look at a person while conversing and arranging chairs around a table) but not competing events (such as to simultaneously carry on a face-to-face and phone conversation).

The Pop-Out Phenomenon is an intriguing element in vigilance. It is the unexpected experience we often have of suddenly recognizing a friend in a large group of people we are merely monitoring. It probably has something to do with unique features our friend has that are not shared by the surrounding people, but this remarkable attentional property is currently ill understood.

As remarkable as our vigilance system is, it is not good at sustaining attention on tasks that are oriented to precise details and contain only subtle environmental shifts. Many educational activities require students to maintain vigilant attention (such as while working a page of similar math problems or studying a text), and teachers often have management problems when they extend these study periods.

Vigilance is an important component in most games children play (from tag to videogames), so they seem to have an almost innate sense that they need to develop the system. It is a good idea, therefore, to create activities that enhance students' abilities to decide whether to maintain a current attentional focus and then to make intelligent choices about short- and long-term attentional tasks.

Our three-part attention system thus moves us from arousal to focus. It is a sort of zoom lens that can zoom in to identify and carefully examine details (foreground), or zoom out to scan the context (background).

Although educators have been especially concerned about ADHD, it is important to realize that it is only one of many mental illnesses and learning handicaps that result from a malfunction in one or more of the subsystems that regulate attention (such as anxiety, autism, bipolar disorder, dyslexia, hyperactivity, mental retardation, obsessive-compulsive disorder, and schizophrenia). Furthermore, many accidents and much classroom misbehavior involve attentional lapses.

Because attentional malfunctions create such serious human problems, it is becoming evident that attention is a more central cognitive system than many thought it to be. Indeed, emotion and attention may be the integrated cognitive system that is most closely related to consciousness, long the Holy Grail of the cognitive neurosciences.

Consciousness involves our subjective awareness of and focus on a small part of the vast amount of information our brain is currently processing, which is pretty much what emotion and attention regulate. Damasio (1999) suggests that consciousness is the key to our subjective recognition of our irresistable biological urge to stay alive and to develop a concern for our own selves and for others. If so, emotion and attention are central to classroom management.

Solve

Solutions to the many internal/external challenges that we confront emerge out of a complex set of interacting conscious/ unconscious neuronal systems that involve such cognitive elements as learning and memory, reason and logic, and a wide range of reflective/reflexive problem-solving strategies. Various theories of intelligence (that combine these cognitive elements) have emerged, and these purport to classify the kinds of problems we confront and the general cognitive strategies we use to solve them.

Because Gardner's (1983, 1998) Theory of Multiple Intelligences is perhaps the best known of these theories among educators, I briefly adapted it below to reflect the functional brain systems that regulate it. To simplify the discussion, I use Gardner's categories as a focus in subsequent chapters that explore (among other things) the classroom management implications of intelligent and nonintelligent behavior. This practical approach should thus serve as a useful parallel to the extensive current literature on the curricular and instructional applications of Gardner's theory.

In so doing, I want to underscore that strong biological correlates exist also for other current excellent widely respected theories of intelligence, such as those of Perkins (1995) and Sternberg (1985).

Reflective Solutions

Some nonthreatening environmental challenges do not require immediate solutions. They focus on life's continuing challenges with our personal/social identity and with natural and electronic space/time. Solutions often emerge slowly, on the basis of a reflective exploration of the factual objective elements of a situation. We can functionally arrange Gardner's nine forms of intelligent reflective response into three sets of three basic identity/space/time problem categories that define human life. The assumption of modularity is that each of these intelligent response systems is processed by (currently ill-understood) dedicated specialized neuronal systems that would be very much interconnected with systems that process the other forms of intelligence.

Intelligence subsystems with an inward focus:

• Who? Personal/Social/Existential Intelligence

Who am I, and who are these people around me? What does it mean to exist? (Gardner: Intrapersonal/Interpersonal/Existential Intelligences.) Chapter 7 (and to an extent Chapter 3) explores the management implications of these concepts.

Intelligence subsystems with an outward focus:

• Where? Space/Place Intelligence

Where am I, and how can I get from here to there? How is nature organized? (Gardner: Spatial/bodily-kinesthetic/naturalist intelligences.) Chapter 4 explores the management implications of these concepts.

• When? Time/Sequence Intelligence

How long has this been going on, what should we do about it, and what will happen if we carry out our plans? (Gardner: Language/Musical/Logical-Mathematical Intelligences.) Chapter 5 explores the management implications of these concepts.

The process of the reflective solution of a problem begins with the past, our learning/memory system that searches for information related to previous similar situations. Learning is how our brain acquires new information, and memory is how and where our brain stores it. Learning/memory is a large part of what we manage in classrooms, so we need to understand it if we hope to manage it.

Scientists generally divide memory into the following systems: (a) a short-term/limited-capacity system called working memory (discussed above) that has no long-term recall, and (b) a more complex long-term memory system that unconsciously processes skills (procedural memory) (such as knowing how to touch-type), and that consciously processes factual label-and-location information (declarative memory).

Scientists further subdivide declarative memory into autobiographical memories of personal experiences (episodic memory) such as our memory of learning how to type, and cultural memories of more abstract and symbolic objects, events, and relationships (semantic memory) such as knowing common elements on all word processors. We further tend to remember when and where specific episodic learning activities took place, but not semantic learning. For example, I remember studying spelling in elementary school, but I do not remember when I learned to spell *accommodate* correctly. So our memory mechanisms are complex, and although still ill-understood, they form the substrate of all curricula, and factual memory formation and recall tend to dominate classroom activity and assessment.

Because emotion is the thermostat that activates the attentional focus that may lead to learning/memory, we create separate emotional memories that help spark the activation (and a subcortical structure called the amygdala appears to play an important role in processing emotional memories). Think of factual memory as being more about remembering *what happened,* and emotional memory as being about remembering *how you felt about what happened.* Both are important, but our emotional memories are the more powerful (our emotional memories of childhood, for example, are stronger than our remembrance of all the factual details of childhood).

Factual memory formation and recall require emotional time and space associations with the various elements of a perceived object or event (such as whether a history fact will be on the test). A factual memory is thus tied to its context and so is easily learned and forgotten. If school requirements are the only context for the material to be learned, it is easily forgotten when we leave school, as all of us have experienced as students. Misbehavior often occurs when students are required to learn things that have no context for (or emotional relationship to) their personal lives.

The following memory metaphor explains and so helps us understand the important relationship between our emotional and factual memories (Sylwester & Margulies, 1998).

When we are overwhelmed by information and/or challenge, we tend to reinvent the related body/brain process outside our body and let that technology carry the load. Examples include phone books, dictionaries, calculators, and photographs. Thus, in our search for a simple explanation for emotional and factual memory, it is useful to metaphorically explore the systems outside our skull that we have developed to store and retrieve complex combinations of information.

The combination of file cabinet, file folders, and files might be a useful metaphor for memory, one that you and your students can easily explore because it has many parallels to what our brain actually does as it gathers, organizes, stores, retrieves, and uses information.

Think of your brain as a reasonably full and useful file cabinet. Think then of an emotional memory as a file folder (within a cabinet drawer) that contains many files, the factual memories of specific objects/events related to the emotion. When you pull out a file folder, you have easy access to all the files in it. When the file folder is in the file cabinet, though, you do not have easy access to the files.

It is useful to limit ready access to many of our factual memories to situations in which we are in the time/space/emotional neighborhood. Imagine a trip to the downtown area of a city you have visited, but not recently. Before going, you may have trouble recalling specific locations, stores, cafes, and so forth, but when you arrive in the area, many factual memories easily return. The emotional state of being there automatically pops out the file folder and you have ready access to the factual information you need.

Imagine the cognitive overload if we had continuous easy access to all such factual memories even when we did not need them, when we were not in the neighborhood. Or think of a class reunion and how we effortlessly recall long-dormant memories of people and events, or the instant recall of prior related negative experiences during an argument with a spouse or friend.

We thus have the best access to weak factual memories (the files) through strong emotional memories (the file folders). Factual memories without emotional context are difficult to store and retrieve. The names/dates/places kinds of curricular information we ask students to remember are a good example. Students often ask, "Will this be on the test?," and if the answer is "Yes," they then have a useful emotional file folder for the information: test things. During the test, they psychologically pull out and use the file folder and its names/dates/places information, but (as indicated above) it is quite problematic if the file folder ever comes out in any nontest situation.

School simulation and role-playing activities thus provide a useful emotional context (or file folder) because they are related to real-life emotional uses of the information. Conversely, multiple choice (and related) tests generally mask the context of factual information. The result is that students often associate the facts with the test rather than with their cultural utility. Students who pass the test may still be unable to use the information in its cultural context.

If the emotional overtones of an experience are very important, we may create especially strong emotional and weak factual memories of the event. Thus, an abused child who must continue to live in an abusive situation may be better off focusing on aversion strategies than on remembering all the details of past abuse. A strong related emotional stimulus years later may then trigger the recall of these weak factual memories (as also occurs with long-dormant school memories at a class reunion) (Kandel & Kandel, 1994).

Mass media, marketers, politicians, and special interest groups often exploit our emotional/factual memory system by hammering us with emotion-laden terms and images that they design to pull out emotional file folders biased to their position. Two such placard-waving groups with opposite views on the issue of Internet censorship regulations recently appeared in the same newspaper picture: one waving a sign with the message "Stop Child Pornography!" and the other "Protect Our First Amendment Rights!" How newspaper readers will contemplate the issue depends somewhat on which file folder popped up in a reader's mind upon seeing the picture and whether the facts supporting the position were seriously biased. Similarly, emotion-laden terms related to such cultural areas as race, ethnicity, gender, religion, and sexual behavior will quickly spark response.

Even if we do not already have an emotional file folder for an issue we confront for the first time (such as the 1997 unexpected announcement of cloning), we tend toward expressing an almost immediate emotional response. Think of the organization of a library. If the book we seek is gone, we usually examine the two adjacent books because libraries are organized so that the two adjacent books are always the closest in focus/content to any shelved book. Similarly, when we confront a novel challenge, our emotional system tends to begin our response sequence with something we consider similar. In the case of cloning, perhaps the Nazi genetic experiments, science fiction, religious beliefs, a love of science, or the novel *Brave New World* initially popped out in your mind.

Reflective solutions thus emerge within the context of our rational analysis of the present problem—an analysis that considers past related remembered experiences and the possible future effects of our decision. Our complex solution systems thus nimbly traverse our human space/time framework: here/there and past/present/future.

A number of programs that purport to teach specific reflective thinking/problem-solving strategies have emerged in recent years and we can expect more. All report success, and so it may well be that it does not make too much difference which approach a program uses as long as it works and complements the focus of the school's curriculum and the comfort level of those who implement it. Student brains tend to resist programs that are not tuned to their cognitive rhythms.

Reflexive Solutions

Threatening or opportunistic challenges often require an immediate response (such as what to do about a rapidly approaching car or how to take advantage of a fleeting opportunity). Our brain has a separate, three-part, stress-driven reflexive system that quickly activates powerful, principally innate, but also learned automatic fight/flight response programs when the emotional impetus is basically to quickly attack, flee, or mate.

Reflexive responses tend to occur on the basis of high emotional arousal and focus and on limited superficial information because we do not have time to gather all the facts. When survival is at stake, a rapid (even if it is not the best possible) response is preferable to informed death from delay.

Rapid reflexive responses may thus save our lives, but they can also unfortunately lead to the stereotyping (such as in racism, sexism, and elitism), regrets, and apologies that are unfortunately so common when we make fearful, impetuous, and ill-informed responses. Worse, the neurotransmitter and hormonal discharges associated with fear can strengthen the emotional and weaken the factual memories of an event if the stressful situation is serious and/or chronic. We become fearful of something but we are often not sure why, so we have learned little from the experience that is consciously useful (because a reflexive response occurs unconsciously and reduces our ability to create factual memories).

Some research evidence suggests that the oversecretion of powerful stress hormones (such as cortisol) that accompanies the chronic activation of our reflexive pathways can physically deteriorate key areas of our factual memory and reflective systems (Sapolsky, 1999). Because the point of a reflexive response is to respond quickly, it is important for our emotion/attention system to turn up the reflexive pathways and to turn down the reflective pathways that would delay the response. The stress hormones enhance the functioning of reflexive pathways, but they can negatively affect the robustness of chronically turned-down reflective pathways.

So what we have is a very powerful and useful stress-driven reflexive response system that should be activated in situations that require an immediate forceful response, such as the sudden accelerations and rapid braking often necessary in averse traffic conditions. The reflexive system evolved, however, to be used as a temporary rather than continuous response system (continuous acceleration and braking when driving is not advisable). Thus, it is like salt, a little bit of it is biologically useful, and a whole lot is generally harmful.

In this light, school students' physical aggression is a continuing problem (especially among males). Chronic aggressors often respond reflexively and aggressively to minor confrontations that do not warrant such a response but the aggressor did not consider alternatives. We are frustrated by such troubling student behavior and tend to seek single, simple explanations—mass media, guns, poor parenting/teaching, chemical imbalances—but behavioral biology is generally more complicated than that.

For example, testosterone has long been a chemical candidate to explain male aggression. It is an important steroid with multiple values. It promotes bone growth and muscle mass, lowers the male voice, and helps develop sexual characteristics. It also binds to brain areas that influence behavior. Both males and females have testosterone, but males have much more than females.

Male testosterone levels surge between 10 and 14 before leveling off, and they fluctuate across the day and year. The folk wisdom thus tagged testosterone as the correlational culprit because male aggression also tends to surge in mid-adolescence. Sapolsky (1998) discovered that it is not that simple. Although all adolescent males experience this adolescent testosterone elevation, not all adolescent males typically respond aggressively to threat.

Two brain structures, the amygdala and hypothalamus, play key roles in activating our rapid reflexive and often assertive response to an imminent danger or opportunity. Elevated testosterone levels do not trigger such an aggressive response but they can turn up the volume of an already triggered reflexive response and so escalate simple anger and assertiveness (which could be used positively in a reflective response) into reflexive physical aggression. So it is not the testosterone that is the culprit but rather that its considerable energy potential is channeled into a reflexive rather than reflective response.

This certainly underscores the importance of helping students to understand and respect the power of their survival-oriented reflexive system and also to develop effective reflective capabilities that can override or compensate for the social problems that reflexive responses often cause. Subsequent chapters will focus on this issue.

Unfortunately, some students live in such an insecure, fearful environment that their reflexive system seems to run continuously. A condition called *learned helplessness* can result from such an environment. The child eventually senses no personal control over an unpredictable environment and simply gives up the innate drive to cope.

It is thus important to remember, when developing curricular and behavior policies and practices, that chronically fearful home and school environments can biologically diminish a student's ability to learn and remember. To create a chronically stressful school environment to increase learning is thus biologically both counterproductive and irresponsible.

Act

Solutions lead to behavior, and behavioral responses are principally mediated by three sets of appendages that constitute the motor system that gives us our mobility—leg, foot, and toe system (for moving); arm, hand, and finger system (for handling); and our neck, mouth, and tongue system (for talking and eating).

Mobility is perhaps our most definitive property. The reason why we have a brain and plants do not is because we can move under our own volition and power and plants cannot. You do not need a brain if you are not going anywhere. A tree that would profit from moving to where there is more sunlight and nutrients is out of luck. Mobility's significance to human life suggests that educative experiences must activate the entire motor system so that we do not merely move but do so with style and grace. Virtuoso movement is central to the visual, aural, and movement arts. Classroom movement tends to focus on one pencil-laden appendage assembling letters and digits on a playing field the size of a sheet of typing paper. We can and should certainly improve on that—creating activities that stimulate and develop a wide range of movement skill. Chapter 6 explores the management implications of this concept.

From Jungle to Classroom
in Search of a Model

So how does our modular plastic brain develop (and apportion space to) the large number of neural networks it needs to operate the specific functional systems and subsystems described throughout this chapter? And an obviously related question (at least for this book) is how do 30 or so people who share a classroom develop the skills to properly apportion energy, space, time, and movement within appropriate ranges to execute the functions society expects of them?

Biological Replication

Edelman (1992) persuasively argues that the evolutionary natural selection processes that shaped our biological environment and basic human brain over long periods of time also shape the developing neural networks of each individual brain over its lifetime. Edelman sees similarities between the rich evolving ecology of a jungle environment and the gradual development of our brain's neural networks. Plants and animals in a jungle area (and neural networks in a brain) function both competitively and symbiotically in response to environmental challenges. The overall result can be a vibrant healthy community, but one that at any given moment also includes opportunity and danger and triumph and tragedy for individual organisms (or neural networks).

The point for an organism is to survive and reproduce. Survival in nature means to locate an ecological niche suited to one's needs and abilities and then to use available energy to gain and protect needed resources and to adapt to changing conditions. Organisms function for their individual survival, not for the good of the species. Those organisms that best adapt to environmental challenges reproduce the most successfully, which may in fact enhance the health of the species but not by deliberate design. Edelman (1992) argues that these same Darwinian principles determine how individual neural networks develop over time. His theory would argue, for example, that differential human abilities and talents would emerge from the development of abnormally large and robust networks in the brain areas that regulate the person's specialty (such as abnormalities in the motor areas that regulate a talented pianist's finger movements).

Cultural Replication

Some scientists further suggest that the same general Darwinian principles govern the cultural replication and evolution of ideas—that many cultural concepts, such as wheels, language, music, clothing, and schools persist across cultures but gradually change over time. Dawkins (1989a) and Blackmore (1999) call these modifiable persistent units of cultural transmission *memes*—analogous to biological genes. They emerge out of the (seemingly unique) ability of humans to imitate the selected cultural behavior of others. For example, children learn how to drink from a cup by observing and copying parental patterns and to speak their native language by copying the speech patterns they hear. We hear a joke and pass it on; we like a clothing style and copy it.

Electronic communication technologies have recently vastly increased our ability to observe and imitate others—well beyond neighborhood confines. We now inhabit a gossipy worldwide electronic village with several hundred million neighbors. The Internet is the ultimate free-for-all in the explosive world of memes.

Mass media unfortunately often mask context, what occurs anywhere is immediately available everywhere, so normal space/time frameworks become confused in the minds of many. For example, a rare and isolated emotionally charged event somewhere can become a rampant phenomenon in the minds of many who followed its extensive media coverage and commentary.

The positive side of this is that it allows us to empathize with people we have never met in person, such as in the wide outpouring of grief that often occurs after a major tragedy. The negative side is that it also leads to the memetic tendency to replicate here what occurred there, and that did occur with the copycat violence and threats of violence after each of the several American school murders that occurred during the final years of this past century. At another, less-violent level, it also continuously occurs in schools as mass media-driven fashions (such as in clothing, speech, and behavior) quickly spread across the land.

Similarly, many instructional and classroom management practices persist and evolve over long periods of time. For example, classrooms (almost by definition) have long tended to have a dominant teacher presence, who apportions resources and directs energy expenditures. Conversely, in a balanced ecological system, no one organ/organism dominates. All elements have opportunities to share in resources, and all make long-term positive contributions (although the prey in an area may not especially appreciate the current contribution of its predators).

We can see an ecological parallel in a balanced modular plastic brain with its many neural networks that operate the functional systems. They must work cooperatively and competitively to enhance the life of the total organism. Each system contributes something important. Mental illness results from the malfunction of one or more important brain system.

We can see a similar ecological parallel in a democratic society that distributes governance and resources among its citizens, with elected leaders who are answerable to the electorate. Our schools have a major responsibility to develop democratic knowledge, attitudes, and skills in students that will allow them to participate productively, and so we have seen a move toward more democratic classroom management procedures in recent decades; but we are still faced with a fundamental inconsistency between the perceived needs of adult society for efficient, effectively managed schools and the needs of students for a laboratory to explore democratic policies and practices.

When we begin to think biologically and ecologically, we discover that the classroom management arena provides an excellent laboratory setting for such democratic activity and beyond. Current classroom behavior and misbehavior can actually become important elements of the curriculum. An imaginative class can explore parallels between a playground skirmish and a national war, between class and community cooperative projects. In the process, they will also discover parallels between life in a classroom and life in an ecological area, such as a jungle or prairie.

This is not a new or revolutionary idea. It is a tenet of existing democratic classroom management programs. What such mental exploration does is to begin the process of connecting elements of biology and classroom management. Such thinking leads to the realization that key concepts in biology and ecology are not any more arcane than day-to-day life in a classroom. They are fundamental, grounded in common sense. Modular plastic brains in a modular adaptable classroom. How exciting!

Chapter ❸

Expending Energy:
Who's in Charge

●━━━━━━━━━━━━━━━━━━━━━━━━━●

Energy is the elusive concept that drives all life. When we expend energy in the limited space/time world that we inhabit, movement generally occurs. Energy, space, time, and limited movement are thus key elements of human life, and so they are also key elements in classroom management. Classrooms and their occupants are about *space*, the school year and its schedules and rhythms are about *time*, potential/kinetic *energy* is about behavior (and its antecedents and effects), and behavior causes physical and psychological *movement* within limited biological and cultural *ranges*.

Because everything begins with energy, this chapter explores the biological and classroom management implications of biological and cultural energy (and the four chapters that follow focus in turn on space, time, movement, and range). The concept of energy encompasses a mixed bag of subconcepts with important classroom management implications such as emotion, attention, self-concept and self-esteem, interest, motivation, ability, funding, control, rules, and assessment. This chapter explains biological and cultural energy, defines key management issues, and suggests metaphors and activities that could help a class (or staff) begin the task of devising a classroom management program that can tie current and potential thought about classroom management to related developments in biology (and especially in the cognitive neurosciences). The subsequent chapters on space, time, movement, and range provide similarly useful program development resource ideas and materials.

> If you are a classroom teacher, consider using the material in this book in the development of an instructional unit for the beginning of the school year. The unit could (a) introduce your students to the organization, development, and management of their individual and collective bodybrains; and (b) explore how they can best use this understanding of themselves to create a comfortably effective classroom management program.

Chapter 2 ended with Edelman's (1992) jungle metaphor related to the development and operation of our bodybrain. It suggests that just as no one organism continually controls a rich ecological environment, so no one biological system continually controls our bodybrain. Rather, our various systems continually shift in their relative level of importance and in the control they exert over other systems.

Institutions are similar. For example, we tend to think of the fire chief as the one who controls the fire department, but it is the person who just turned in an alarm who determines the department's next action; the student who hit another student (at least momentarily) controls things in the classroom. The issue of who or what controls the classroom (mostly and currently) is thus fundamental to any discussion about the design and implementation of a classroom management model for the 21st century. It is where to begin, and so what follows is a metaphorical issue that might enhance such an exploration.

Childbirth, Childhood, and Classrooms

Chapter 1 suggested that we can think of a class in a classroom as a living social organism. Its metaphoric properties include the semipermeable membranes, unorganized nutrient materials, and organizing agent that characterizes life at various levels. We humans have about a couple dozen organs in our body, and a classroom has about a couple dozen inhabitants. To extend the metaphor, we could think of school as a reproductive act. The adult culture defines itself in curricular terms that it seeks to instill into the next generation, gathered into classroom groups. Let us explore classroom management in this context through two intriguing contradictory perspectives, each with considerable support in our society.

The Classroom as a Womb

The school year in the United States is about 9 months long, which is about the gestation period of a human fetus. A womb is a warm, supportive, nutritionally controlled environment. The embryo/fetus does not make any of the conscious decisions during the pregnancy, although in time the mother can sense its responses to what is occurring and possibly adjust things. It is in the mother's best interests to be responsible in decisions that affect her pregnancy. To injure her developing fetus with drugs, for example, results in a harsh biological judgment and punishment—she must rear the child she injured.

Many people think of a classroom as something like a nurturing womb, a controlled environment in which an immature social organism (the class) gradually develops toward the more independent level of birth (the class graduates). An instructional umbilical cord that connects society to the classroom supplies the needed curricular nutrients during development.

This perspective suggests that students are by definition immature in important knowledge and skills, and so it is in society's and the students' best interests for the teacher to carefully control the classroom environment, to shield students from the harsh education they would get if they had to get it all on their own within the community. Classroom walls keep students from wandering cluelessly in the traffic. This perspective sees formal education as an expensive and significant element of enculturation, and argues that our society cannot afford to make errors in its operation by encouraging or allowing immature students to control things. Even Dewey (1938), the founder of Progressive Education, argued that it was foolish to assign mature adults to work in classrooms with immature students and then not use their maturity to enhance the students' experience.

In such an adult-controlled nurturing setting, the class (as a dependent social organism) can develop positively in its knowledge and skills during the 9-month school year and emerge from its classroom womb on a spring day into the birth of a joyful, independent summer vacation. Three months later, groups of students will crawl back into another classroom womb, repeat the process, and mature a little more. They will eventually graduate and become productive adults.

The Class as an Independent Social Organism

Not so, argue the critics of the classroom-as-a-womb perspective. These critics do not consider a class to be a dependent entity but rather a living functioning social organism, and they believe that the classroom setting should encourage the free exploration of much of what life is about. Such a class was conceived as a social organism in the principal's office in late summer from the school's genetic pool (the student files) and was born the day after, Labor Day (in many communities), to live a rich 9-month life. The class will inevitably die as a social organism on the final day of school, with practically no chance of coming together again intact in subsequent school years. A class has a 9-month life and a charge to make the most of it.

Social development is a principal task of the school, and so this perspective argues that the school should encourage a class to chart its own social and problem-solving development as much as possible. It should discover how to make the best use of each student, just as our bodybrain has to get all its organs and systems to function cooperatively.

We could think of the school year as a life that includes an early autumn childhood in which the class begins to feel its own way with a lot of encouragement and support from the teacher (just as parents play a similarly important role in a child's early maturation). We could think of the extended middle months as analogous to a productive adult life in which the group assumes much more control over its affairs. We could think of the spring months as analogous to the senior, more reflective years of life. It is an opportunity to look back to see how far we have come and what we have accomplished. In a classroom group, this period can become an important time for individual students to solidify relationships and to set their agenda for subsequent years. Who was I? Who am I? Who will I become?

This classroom management perspective argues that the only way for students to master social and problem-solving skills is to explore and practice them with as much independence as possible. To have the teacher and curriculum teach these skills via lesson format is not as powerful as having students discover them, and as long as the teacher monitors such issues as safety and legality, the classroom orientation should be to foster social and problem-solving independence. The teacher must obviously play the same dominant role that a parent plays during infancy, to help get the group started; but once the school year is under way, the teacher should take every possible opportunity to let the class group determine its own way, to identify and solve its own social problems. This perspective strongly believes in the ancient adage that the teacher must decrease in importance over time so that the students may increase in importance.

So which perspective is correct? When we look to biology for guidance, we can see support for a nurturing dependency—the coverings around nuts, bird nests to shelter eggs covered by eggshells, the chrysalis covering of the insect pupal stage, the mammalian womb. We can also see support for early exploratory independence; most animals are on their own shortly after birth, innately tuned to survival in the environment in which they will live.

A womb-like classroom's strengths are in helping individual students discover what others think of me, how the environment shapes me, and how to function appropriately within a group. Its goal is to get the class through the year's curricular expectations.

An exploratory classroom's strengths are in helping individual students to discover what I/we think, how we can best shape our own classroom environment, and how we can best evolve as a functioning group. Its goal is to get the class simply to experience the year for what it is.

The goals seem contradictory, but many teachers try to combine them. For example, they take a nurturing womb approach during skill development activities (such as in reading and math computation) and an exploratory approach during such activities as the arts and humanities and in planning classroom events.

Problems emerge. What happens if students go through a year in which their teacher encourages them to work together on many things, and they develop the skills of independent social action, and the following year most are assigned to a teacher who tightly controls classroom life? What happens when a new student joins a class that has spent months developing a productive group identity, and the new student has difficulty in participating in such activities? What happens in a school in which the staff prefers the exploratory perspective, but students come and go so much that the spring student body is considerably different from the student body of the previous fall. Furthermore, students in a departmentalized school may experience a range of management perspectives during the course of a single day because the staff differ significantly in their beliefs about classroom management (something easily discovered when staff discuss these two perspectives and then votes their personal orientation).

It is obvious that one can make a very good case for either perspective, and both perspectives have considerable support within our profession and among our patrons. It is thus a useful metaphor to begin the exploration of whether the teacher or the students should make the principal expenditure of energy in determining how classroom management decisions should be made across the school year.

Unfortunately, metaphors are much better at defining problems than at providing easy solutions, but they do enhance the discussions that lead to solutions, and I certainly wish you well in that important initial exercise.

From Potential to Kinetic Energy

The issue of who should expend the energy to determine and execute classroom management policies and procedures might be dependent, at least to some extent, on the nature and wishes of individual students and the nature of the class group. One could argue that students who are quite immature will need more professional direction than more mature students. Conversely, an elementary class with 1,000 hours over 9 months at its disposal has more time to gradually develop and determine its social organization than a secondary school departmentalized class that meets only 45 minutes a day for 12 weeks (about 45 hours). One can also argue that because we are born into a democratic society, the process of social self-management should be introduced as early as possible.

The issue occurs at all levels. I can recall (as both student and teacher) marvelous graduate seminars in which the students organized and ran the course, and I can recall being a student in marvelous courses in which I did not want to spend class time on such management issues but, rather, preferred to assimilate as much as possible of the professor's superior knowledge of a subject that I wanted to master. I also know that not all students in a graduate seminar want to run things and not all students in a lecture course want to be lectured at, even by a superstar in the field.

So it might come down to the simple question of what part of the school experience emotionally arouses (or challenges) a student. Emotion and attention are our activation systems, and Chapter 2 suggested that arousal is mediated by the effects of long-term temperament, short-term mood, and immediate emotional needs—a rich stew pot indeed.

As indicated earlier, we are a social species, continually cooperating and competing with each other. We are stimulated by activities that involve both, for example, in business by debate and negotiation and in play by games such as basketball and bridge. What determines when we prefer to use our energy to compete or to cooperate? The answer emerges partly out of our human ability to assess ourselves and others in social situations, and so to determine the personal payoff for competition or cooperation. Recent evolutionary psychology research on aggressive behavior and the related concepts of self-concept (how I define myself) and self-esteem (how I value that definition) provide an intriguing biological perspective of the possible source of a student's desire to positively participate in or to negatively oppose the management of a class.

So in the discussion that follows, think of self-concept/self-esteem as a basic energizing force that helps drive emotion (which drives attention, problem solving, and behavior). It is therefore something that we need to understand as we wrestle with the issue of who should manage the classroom.

Self-Esteem, Impulsivity, and Aggression

Impulsive behavior can lead to reckless behavior, which can lead to violently aggressive behavior. Thus many personal and social problems begin with an impulsive act that is triggered (at least in part) by the aggressor's level of self-esteem.

Our extended maturation and relatively long life span turned us into an interdependent social species. We are thus rightly concerned that efforts and resources are equitably distributed within our formal and informal groups and that hostility among members is minimized. We compete for individual success with the available resources, but our individual success often depends on our ability to function cooperatively within the social hierarchy of the group.

The following two intriguing questions focus on how our cognitive systems developed to solve such social management problems: (a) How did our brain develop its ability to function effectively and contentedly within a hierarchical social setting, and (b) which brain systems regulate and trigger our variable social responses, from altruism to aggression?

These are important societal and classroom management questions because if genetics and biochemical systems combine to trigger aggression, for example, one could argue that chronically aggressive people have a reduced capacity for free will and thus should not be held as responsible for their acts as others are. Furthermore, if courts mandate (and/or schools encourage) medical treatments for people who behave inappropriately, the policy could be viewed as governmental mind control, racism, or elitism. The social implications of this research and the policies that will emerge out of it are profound and wide ranging. For example, when determining legal or classroom responsibility for an aggressive act, should we simply consider the behavior to be wrong, or should we factor in negative effects of the aggressor's life experiences and environment and the specific event(s) that triggered the aggression?

Brain Systems

Our modular brain's complex collections of neural networks process our cognitive activity. Individual networks that process specific functions combine to process more complex functions. Several dozen neurotransmitter and hormonal systems provide the key chemical substrate of this marvelous information-processing system. Neurotransmitter molecules produced within one neuron are released from its axon (output) terminal into the synaptic gap, where they cross over and attach to (input) receptors on the dendrites or cellular surface of the next neuron in the information sequence. Each neuron produces one or two types of neurotransmitters.

Recent studies with human and nonhuman primates suggest that fluctuations in the availability of the neurotransmitter serotonin play an especially important role in regulating our level of self-esteem and our place within the social hierarchy. Researchers associate high serotonin levels with high self-esteem and social status, and low serotonin levels with low self-esteem and social status. Behaviorally, high serotonin levels are associated with the calm assurance that leads to smoothly controlled movements, and low serotonin levels are associated with the irritability that leads to impulsive, uncontrolled, reckless, aggressive, violent, suicidal behaviors that are often directed toward inappropriate targets. Serotonin levels also seem to affect attention deficit (ADD, ADHD) and other movement-related school behavioral disorders.

It is adaptive for a social species to develop a system that arranges groups into reasonably compatible hierarchical arrangements to better perform various group tasks (and especially those over evolutionary time that involved skilled movements). The entire group benefits if survival-related tasks are assigned to those who are generally recognized to be the most capable. As indicated above, self-concept thus emerged to provide us with a sense of how we define ourselves relative to others, and self-esteem emerged to determine how we value that definition. These judgments help us determine our strengths and weaknesses and encourage us to strive within the group. Consider the personal/skill factors involved in the choice sequence when children choose sides for teams.

Wright (1995) suggests that the social feedback we get from our actions creates fluctuations from our basal serotonin levels, and this helps us determine our current level of self-esteem. Thus serotonin fluctuations are adaptive in that they help primates negotiate social hierarchies, move up as far as circumstances permit, and be reasonably content at each stage. Social success elevates our self-esteem (and serotonin levels), and each such success further raises our social expectations, perhaps to try for a promotion or leadership role we had not considered when we were lower on the hierarchy.

A biological system of variability in self-esteem prepares and encourages us to reach and maintain a realistic level of social status, given our abilities and the group's composition. A high or low level of self-esteem (and serotonin) is not innate and permanent. Very successful people may tumble precipitously in social status, self-esteem, and serotonin levels when they retire or are discharged, and they thereby experience a rapid reduction in positive social feedback.

This does not mean that the serotonin system developed to help low-status people endure their fate for the common good. Evolutionary psychology argues that natural selection rarely designs things for the good of the group. What the serotonin system does do is provide us with a way to cope psychologically in a bad social situation—to be content to play a group role that is consistent with one's current limitations.

The Peter Principle wryly argues that bureaucracies generally suffer from a high level of incompetence because employees tend to be promoted one level beyond their level of competence. At that point, promotions cease because of negative performance feedback, and the tenured employee settles into a career of barely getting by until retirement.

Males (normatively) seem to value competition and the development and maintenance of social hierarchies more than females. Although it is currently an ill-understood issue, evolutionary psychologists suggest that this tendency may have emerged out of gender differences in reproductive needs and strategies and possibly out of the role differentiations of hunting parties, but gender group differences do not predict the behavior of individual males and females. The human serotonin system seems to function similarly in males and females in the important roles it plays in regulating self-esteem and aggression control.

The Roots of Violence and Aggression

Violent and aggressive acts are very distressing to the victims and are prominently featured in the news and mass media, but they are not the norm in social interactions. Furthermore, young males commit most of such acts, and 7% of the population commits 80%

of the acts. Thus violence and aggression are a limited social pathology, one that evolutionary psychologists seek to explain. Consider the following scenario: A young man goes out for football in his freshman high school year. He is thrilled just to make the team, even though he knows he is low on the hierarchy and will not get to play much in games. He is content for now because he also knows that the coaches and his teammates will note every successful act he makes in scrimmage, and so his playing time will come.

Evolutionary psychology argues that each success enhances his serotonin level and so also his motor coordination and self-esteem. He moves up the team hierarchy, substituting for a few minutes in games. His competition for most of his journey is not the alpha males at the top of the hierarchy but, rather, those who are competing with him for the next slot on the team hierarchy. Over several years his talent and that of his teammates will determine the level he achieves. He may thus settle for 4 years of comradeship, scrimmage, and limited game time because he realizes that is where he properly fits in on the team hierarchy, or he may eventually bask in the celebrity afforded him as one of the team stars. If the latter, he may begin the sequence anew on a college team and then perhaps again on a professional team. If the former, his memories and friendships will have to suffice, and he will seek success in other social areas.

But what if he believes that he is better than others who get to play more, but the coaches do not agree and will not give him a proper chance to play? Perhaps it is because of something he cannot control (such as his height), or else he believes that his main competitor for his position gets to play more because he is the son of the coach's best friend. Imagine his frustration and rage. His opportunities do not match his sense of self. Consider also how people feel when such artificial factors as gender, race, ethnicity, and age are used to limit their ability to compete in a wide range of social and vocational settings.

Evolutionary psychologists suggest that this cognitive drive to move into our expected slot on the hierarchy is so strong that many will do whatever it takes to achieve success, and if the frustration becomes too intense, a person may act impulsively, recklessly, and stupidly for any possible chance of success, and such reflexive risk taking may on occasion escalate into aggressive and violent acts. A world-class figure skater even attempted to ensure her status by conspiring to injure the knees of a highly ranked rival Olympic Games competitor.

When young people find themselves in a situation in which they see no hope to rise within mainstream society, they may create their own hierarchical gang cultures (and classroom cliques) that provide them with opportunities to succeed within their counter-culture's mores. Those among the mainstream successful who de-cry gang symbols and exclusionary turf areas should look to the high-status symbols they use to flaunt their success, and to their exclusionary golf courses and walled communities. Are our soci-ety's mainstream culture and counterculture that different biologi-cally in terms of a need for a positive self-concept and self-esteem— for recognition that they are players in important areas of their life?

In primate groups with a developed stable hierarchy, those at the bottom (who had little control over events) experienced far more stress and stress-related illness than those at the top. Con-versely, during periods in which the hierarchical structure was unstable and shifting, those currently at the top (whose power was threatened) experienced the most stress and stress-related illness (Sapolsky, 1999). Thus it is in the interest of the power elite (in com-munity and classroom) to maintain social stability, and it is in the interest of the currently disenfranchised to create as much social instability (and classroom disruption) as possible in a desperate search for respect and success.

The fewer opportunities young people have to succeed in mainstream society and the classroom, the more social instability we can expect. It is not in our nation's interest to support ex-clusionary policies that limit social goals, reducing the powerful role that schools play in helping students seek their dreams. The classroom can be an important laboratory for this process.

The Role of Drugs and Nutrition

Is it possible to chemically jump-start the serotonin system when conditions have become so averse in a person's life that self-esteem and serotonin levels have plummeted into the depths of de-pression? Fluoxetine antidepressant drugs such as Prozac, Zoloft, and Paxil can do this. When neurotransmitters leave an axon termi-nal, they attach to a receptor on the receiving neuron and pass on the sending neuron's chemical message. Most are then reabsorbed into the axon terminal and used again. Drugs such as Prozac block the re-uptake channels on the terminal and so slow the reabsorption process. This means that the serotonin neurotransmitters in the synapse may activate several times before being reabsorbed, and so fluoexitine drugs increase the effectiveness of a limited discharge of serotonin without actually increasing the amount in our brain. Such herbal remedies as St. John's Wort also often successfully elevate serotonin levels in people whose levels are moderately low.

This somewhat artificial chemical elevation often enhances a person's motor competence and self-esteem, and this increased optimism and happier mood leads to the positive social feedback that allows the natural system to take over again in time and to function more effectively. Think of jump-starting a dead car battery—a few miles of driving will reenergize the battery, and it can then function on its own.

When researchers physically removed the dominant male from a troop of vervet monkeys and gave fluoexitine antidepressant drugs to a randomly selected lower ranking male, that male assumed a dominant role (Nesse & Williams, 1994).

People often use alcohol when they feel low, and alcohol does release more serotonin into the synapses. It can thus temporally help to raise one's mood and self-esteem, but chronic alcohol use depletes the brain's store of serotonin, and so it makes matters even worse by further impairing the impulse control system.

Nutrition may provide another avenue to serotonin elevation. Serotonin is derived from the amino acid *tryptophan*. Carbohydrates enhance the entry of tryptophan into our brain. Prolonged periods of stress increase our brain's need for serotonin. Nutrition researchers have discovered a connection between serotonin/carbohydrate levels and emotionally driven eating disorders that emerge out of family stress, premenstrual syndrome, shift work, seasonal mood changes, and the decision to stop smoking. Wurtman and Suffes (1996) propose nondrug diet adaptations that could solve some of these problems.

It is interesting that we humans have long self-medicated ourselves with alcohol and carbohydrates (sweets and starches) to temporarily and artificially boost our self-esteem, and Friday afternoon margaritas and chips after a difficult, depressing week seemingly provide a double boost.

From Positive Social Feedback to Classroom Management

Prescription and other drugs can provide only a temporary chemical boost in the energy of self-esteem, and diets require a certain level of self-control. The best support for a serotonin deficiency is probably the natural system of activity and positive social feedback that we have evolved over millennia. Werner and Smith (1992) have conducted a four-decade longitudinal study of seriously at-risk children who matured into resilient, successful adults. The authors found that the children received unconditional love from family and/or nonfamily mentors who encouraged their curiosity, interests, and dreams and who assigned them responsibilities that helped them discover their strengths and weaknesses.

Kays (1990) discovered that an important factor in the alienation from school that many Grades 4 and 5 at-risk students were beginning to feel occurred because their teachers did not involve them in many routine classroom tasks. Other students were asked to water the plants and get things from the office, but not the at-risk students. How can students learn responsibility if they are not asked to be responsible in simple chores?

If both an inexperienced substitute football player and the team's star can work together comfortably and effectively, a cooperative classroom spirit can similarly become a powerful energizing tool for helping a class to enhance its collective self-concept/self-esteem. Serotonin research thus adds biological support to some educational practices that can help develop the skills a class needs to participate responsibly and effectively in the management of its classroom. The suggestions that follow should encourage staff and students to begin the self-examination that is necessary to determine who should do what.

Suggested Activities

Data Gathering

Simple data-gathering activities about such things as how the class feels about something or how much energy an activity took can provide useful information for class discussions about a variety of management issues.

Consistently use a simple 5- or 10-point high-low scale to informally gather data (10 or 5 is high, 1 is low, with the other numbers representing intermediate values). Such a scale quickly gets an honest and easily computed response range from the entire group, and this provides substance to any discussion about what is occurring or what should occur. If secrecy is important, ask students to write the number that represents their opinion on a small slip of paper, gather the slips, and quickly tabulate them on the chalkboard and collectively analyze the group's response. If secrecy is not important, ask students to write down the number on any sheet of paper on their desk and then ask them to hold up their sheet when the tabulator calls out the individual numbers on the scale. (Writing down the number encourages students to stay with their original choice when the scale numbers are called out and not to change an opinion to match that of a friend.) Consider the following data-gathering suggestions that move from immediate to extended data gathering, and then work with your class to develop other activities that fit your situation.

- Begin the day or an activity by asking students to indicate how they currently feel (on a good-bad scale) or their energy or interest level (on a high-low scale).
- At the end of an activity or end of the day, ask students to use the scale to indicate how they felt the activity or day went.
- After a written activity, ask students to place a number on the top of the page to indicate how much energy they expended to compete the assignment, or how confident they are of their success in completing it, their level of interest in the activity, and so forth. Tabulate the numbers and begin the next day's discussion of the assignment with a discussion of the results.
- Record and graph daily student stress levels for at least 2 weeks. When students first enter the classroom each day, ask them to write a number that represents their perceived stress level on a slip of paper and then drop the slip in a box. Place each day's slips in a sealed envelope, labeled with the day. Also keep a daily record of notable events such as weather changes, arguments, and management problems that occurred. After 2 or more weeks, work as a class to tabulate, compute, and graph the daily average results for the entire period. Note and discuss patterns and fluctuations during

the period, and use the record of daily events to explain high and low days, variations during a week, and so on. What effect does the morning assessment have on what happens during the course of the day? What might the group do to reduce negative effects? It is important to gather all the data before analyzing any of it so that each day's assessment does not affect the next day's during the study period.

In an extended informal middle school study of daily stress levels (that used a 10-point scale), one of my graduate students discovered that the data predicted weather changes (with a large fluctuation in perceived stress levels occurring a day or so before the weather changed). He also found that the scores on a given day tended to converge around the teacher's personal score of the previous day (not surprising, because if a teacher feels stressed on Tuesday, the students will not come to school on Wednesday with a whole lot of optimism).

- Ask three students to sit apart at locations where they can easily observe what is going on. At the conclusion of every minute for an hour, each student should write down a subjective assessment of how much positive energy was collectively being expended in the classroom (10 = *very much*, 1 = *very little*). At the end of the hour, ask the students to graph their 60 observations on a graph or graphs that allow for easy comparison. Collectively compare and discuss the three assessments of the same hour.

Using Common Activities to Explore and Enhance Classroom Energy

- When students have many opportunities to work together in groups, they may experience success in both leading and supporting roles, an important developmental consideration for bold/uninhibited and anxious/inhibited temperaments. Positive self-esteem can develop at any level in a work group if the problem is challenging and the group values the contributions of all. The emergence of Cooperative Learning Strategies in recent years has provided educators a useful vehicle for helping students to explore and expand themselves.

- Portfolio assessments are another excellent vehicle for encouraging the self-examination in students that enhances their self-concept and self-esteem. Journals, creative artwork, and other forms of reflective thought can produce similar results.
- Many classroom conflicts arise because an impulsive act escalates into aggression. We have tended to view these events only in negative terms—as misbehavior, as something to be squashed. What if we used positive group strategies to help students study such behavior and discover how to reduce it? Students can then use their own behavior in a classroom laboratory self-study of social behavior.

Many teachers begin the school year with a somewhat arbitrary posting-of-the-rules that will govern classroom behavior. Another more cooperative approach would be to take the time to list and discuss the wide variety of people who expend energy to determine events and behavior in a complex institution such as a school and then to cooperatively seek to determine who should decide what and why.

So title the activity across the top of the chalkboard "Who Decides What and Why?" Under this, horizontally write the following decision-making category levels so that students can suggest and write specific activities under each category (and you can then add things that they do not know or cannot think of):

- Beyond the Building Level
- At the Building Level by Others
- At the Classroom Level by the Teacher
- At the Classroom Level by Teacher and Students
- At the Classroom Level by Individual Students

Decisions beyond the building level involve such things as laws, personnel decisions, funding, busing, and snow days. General building- level decisions involve such things as lunch, library, and gym schedules; classroom assignments; and aide assignments. Teacher decisions might involve such things as the day's schedule, curricular assignments, desk arrangements, and the condition of the room at the end of the day. Teacher/student decisions might involve such things as class projects and parties. Individual student decisions involve such things as what to read during a free reading period, personal thoughts, and friendships. It is always interesting to discover what a class group will identify.

When the listing is complete, work as a group to identify (with an X) those items that the class feels should be negotiable, things that others typically decide but that they believe should be decided with student input. Then, circle those items that the class actually wants to expend the energy to negotiate and/or to control decisions.

It will be an interesting discussion. Your class will discover while working through the activity that no one person controls all the decision making in a school and that legal/safety issues, perceived community consensus, available funding, and a variety of other factors must be considered when making almost all decisions. Even if a teacher insists that a student should do something, *misbehavior* is a term that suggests limitations in teacher authority. It takes a lot of cooperative energy to run a classroom and school, and that is a very good lesson to teach and learn at the beginning of the year.

Chapter ❹

Creating Biological and Cultural Space

●————————————————————————●

Space is an important cognitive concept: here and there, in and out, up and down, big and little, fat and thin, flat and hilly. We are born capable of learning how to successfully solve basic spatial problems in our immediate environment—how to move toward opportunities and away from dangers—and we spend much of our life physically and mentally exploring our planet.

Three of Gardner's (1983, 1998) nine forms of intelligence focus on space: spatial (visual perception and re-creation abilities), bodily-kinesthetic (body motion and navigation abilities), and naturalist (object classification abilities). Knowing how to manage space is thus a very important issue for one brain and also for a classroom of bodybrains. For somewhat simple starters, how does a modular brain arrange its various interactive neural networks within its skull, and how does a class arrange its interactive set of living and nonliving things within its classroom?

The more difficult problems are to discover why some brain and classroom spatial elements are curiously arranged, and how spatial organization affects behavior. In our brain, for example, body movements are principally controlled by a narrow band of cortex that stretches over our brain from ear to ear. Curiously, the motor cortex section in each hemisphere controls movements on the opposite side of our body, and our body areas are arrayed upside down along the motor cortex (the motor areas at the top of our brain control our feet, and the areas near our ears control facial movement). Strange brain geography!

Classroom geography can also sometimes be strange. An elementary teacher once told me that she always gathers her class into a circle at the end of the last school day of the month to discuss how the month had gone and what they might do during the next month. She calls one segment of this session *curiosities,* during which she asks students to identify things that seemed odd, not quite right. She has discovered that periodically someone will identify something reasonably important that she and others had not noticed.

One year at the end of October, a student remarked that the teacher had the biggest desk in the room and it was arranged so that her total area took up a lot of classroom space (as much as several student desks). Furthermore, her desk was located in the best spot in the room (with a great view of the mountains), and yet she never used it during the day. So the issue was, in effect, why did she get the most and best real estate in the room and didn't even use it? The teacher had been teaching for years and had never realized what her student had observed. The result was that she asked her class to help her move her desk into the corner with the lowest real estate value, thus freeing up a lot of classroom space. They then worked out a revolving schedule that allowed three students each month to temporarily move into the prime real estate area with the great view.

Brains and classrooms contain spatial curiosities that often pass us by unless we tune in to their possibility. This chapter thus suggests ideas and offers examples and metaphors related to four spatial aspects of classroom life and management with the hope that they will spark the kind of data gathering, discussion, and design activities that will enhance the understanding and management of classroom space.

1. Objects occupy space, whether they are neurons in a brain or desks in a classroom. Sometimes location is not important (such as the location of a single rock in a rocky area), but location is often quite important to the success of living things in highly competitive settings (such as the location of a tree in a forest or of a cafe in a business district). Where a table or a student is located in a classroom may or may not be important. The general issue of location brings

to mind the two classic approaches to housekeeping. The one approach is that there is a logical place for everything, and everything should be in its place; the other is that wherever a thing is, that is where it was destined to be.

2. A class group is generally surrounded by a leaky wall—a semipermeable membrane. Membranes and their channels (such as classroom walls and doors) participate in the creation of vibrant internal life forces and then disperse the resulting products and behaviors. To create something very vibrant within a classroom is different from merely constructing it. We can only appreciate constructed things (that followed an established set of directions) when they are complete, but we can imagine and appreciate created things (such as a class, classroom, curriculum, or a school year) before, during, and after their creation. The challenge is to create a stimulating classroom environment within the spatial limitations of an already existing school and its policies.

3. Considerable evidence suggests that a stimulating complex social environment enhances the physical development of the cortex, the part of our brain that processes much of the curriculum (Diamond & Hopson, 1998). The nonliving spatial elements of the classroom, such as its walls, furniture, and materials can also materially enhance the creation of a stimulating environment if the inhabitants imaginatively arrange it.

4. Two dozen or so people share a limited classroom space, so classroom management policies and practices should respect everyone's fundamental constitutional right to privacy and due process and to our human right to a safe teaching and learning environment.

Let us begin our exploration of classroom space with the concept of a map because maps (and architectural plans, musical scores, equations, etc.) allow us to mentally imagine things that are physically quite complicated.

Mapping Cognitive, City, and Classroom Space

A brain imaging machine looks down on the deeply folded, approximately 3-square-foot cortex of our modular brain. It images (identifies) individual brain areas that briefly activate as they participate in processing the cognitive tasks that currently engage the person being imaged (typically using the sequence of colors in the spectrum to register variations in activity in various imaged areas: red = high to purple = low activity). Each brain area specializes in a specific aspect of the myriad of actions that the brain can carry out, and each area connects to and influences the actions of many other areas, the aggregate of all the small-to-large activated areas collaborating to process the task at hand. Scientists who study brain scans are learning much about the spatial organization of our modular brain, but the underlying biological logic and management of the system remain elusive (the motor cortex discussed above being an intriguing example).

Now let us think of spending a day hovering over a mid-size city in a helicopter. We would note similarities in observing the behavior of 100 billion neurons and 100,000 citizens. From the helicopter, we might first note the smaller, lifeless geometric shapes that constitute homes and buildings. We would also recognize larger, less clearly defined spatial configurations that constitute such things as industrial, business, and governmental areas; shopping malls; and the neighborhoods with their collections of schools, churches, parks, and business/professional areas. We might also be able to determine that some city areas are composed mostly of old buildings and others of new buildings.

Connecting all these smaller and larger spatial entities are the city's inner complex of streets, roads, freeways, and bridges and the rivers, airport, and highway systems that allow things to move in and out of the city. Not visible but important are the underground wires and pipes.

We would note that some intersecting streets do not connect easily, and some areas and structures seem curiously misplaced (such as a beautiful, large old church in a now shabby partially industrial neighborhood). A city's landscape constantly shifts, and because it is difficult to move or redesign some things, it is sometimes best to just adapt things to the current inadequate spatial arrangement in cities, classrooms, and evolving brains.

During the course of the day we would note fluctuations in the activity levels of various areas and in the arterial ribbons that move people. These might include the morning and afternoon movements between individual homes and the business, industrial, and governmental areas and heightened evening activity in the entertainment and shopping centers. We could assess the amount of activity in a shopping mall, for example, by noting the number of cars parked in its parking lot, and the rhythm of a school day by observing such things as the current presence or absence of students in the play areas and buses out front. The amount of activity an area engenders might be an indication of its importance to the operation of the city.

If we could look closer into all those buildings and track the activity patterns, we would discover that the 100,000 citizens each have an individual permanent home base from which they periodically move to such temporary spaces as schools, jobs, stores, churches, and restaurants. So, for example, students with their own room in a shared home spend school days at a private desk in a shared classroom and school, periodically moving to such temporary spaces as a library or cafeteria table. The student's current personal space may also constantly shift, such as during a physical education activity or when moving about the classroom.

Each citizen (or student) is thus an individual space-filling energy module in a city (or classroom) composed of lifeless private and shared space that comes alive when people act and communicate. Folks constantly move here and there to participate in the temporary increase in an area's activity.

City and classroom space utilization thus have intriguing similarities to brain space utilization. Each function in our modular brain occupies its own (localized or distributed) space, but successful brain activity depends on the collaborative and competitive efforts of many brain modules, just as cities and classrooms function best through an appropriate collaborative/competitive mix.

This suggests that a class could profitably imagine the helicopter view of its school and classroom across the school day and study how school space is used to locate and to move things. Physical closeness and spatial ownership are two intriguing concepts that will probably emerge during the study, and the suggestions below should assist in the process.

How Many People Can You Stuff Into a Classroom?

Physical Closeness. It is odd, but we all attend a football game—which is about physical contact—and avoid physical contact with others in attendance, apologizing when accidental contact occurs.

We will crowd into an elevator or bus, but we want different picnic groups in a park to spread out. We will attend a party in a large house with comfortable conversation-friendly seating areas and all crowd into the kitchen to stand and talk. Men and women happily share the same confined space in a restaurant's eating area but not in its restrooms. People who would not walk around town in a skimpy swimsuit will wear it without embarrassment at a pool. The chances are good that we do not interact much with our neighbors but, rather, much more with friends who are scattered all over town.

> How much space does a class need before it feels crowded among friends and exhibits the irritation associated with overcrowding? Find out by getting enough moveable partitions to stretch along one classroom wall. Every day move the partitions one foot toward the center of the room (thus reducing the available space in the room). Move desks and other equipment closer together as the room shrinks, and work together to gather daily data on how the group is responding (such as recording the number of arguments, daily stress levels, etc.). Discover the point at which the class votes to abandon the project because things have become too crowded. Interestingly, some classes have discovered through the activity that a little crowding is not necessarily bad if it frees up classroom space that can then be used (like park space in a city) for activities that are enhanced by the constant availability of the additional space.

Spatial Ownership. We seem to require a sense of defined personal space. Mammals have a powerful tendency to identify, protect, and mark their territory. We observe it when dogs scent trees and shrubs and when homeowners water the hedge on their property line, but perhaps also when the teacher's name is on a classroom door, and when folks use knives or aerosol paint cans to tag and claim ownership of someone else's wall. When we wear signed designer clothing, wedding rings, and convention tags, we voluntarily give up a little of our personal spatial identity to someone else.

Elementary students typically have a school space they can call their own—a desk in *their* classroom. Elementary teachers generally involve their students in decorating and caretaker activities that further provide the class with a sense of personal space owner-ship. Conversely, secondary school students typically have only temporary desks in a series of teacher-oriented classrooms, and many secondary schools have now even removed the lockers that formerly provided their students with a small personal space in the school.

Personal space is so important to us that many secondary students sit at the same desk every time a class meets, and find a place where they can regularly hang out when they are not in class. They may join the school paper staff or some other activity that has a room they can go to, frequent the library (often always sitting at the same table), and/or congregate by their cars in the parking lot or across the street at a convenience store.

The dispossessed in the student body have located no space where they feel a sense of ownership. Is it a surprise that many feel alienated, drop out, and join with their friends to claim ownership of a hang-out space, often in the center of the city (and usually to the intense irritation of nearby businesses)?

We tend not to vandalize our own property, so educators who do not work to create a sense of student spatial identification (or ownership) should not be surprised when students vandalize the school.

Use the scale introduced at the end of Chapter 3 (5 or 10 = *high*, 1 = *low*) to identify the student comfort level with various school areas. Work together to create a form that identifies various school areas (cafeteria, library, office, playground, etc.) and ask students to rate each in terms of how comfortable (safe, happy, etc.) they feel when they are in that area. Tabulate the results and discuss the response patterns, especially those of the areas students rated highest and lowest.

A Classroom Is a
Created World Surrounded by a Leaky Wall

Chapter 1 identified the semipermeable membrane as a key biological concept. In the context of this chapter, we can think of our protective skull and our brain's sensory/motor inputs and outputs but also of the classroom's barriers (walls, floor, ceiling) and it openings (door, windows, faucets, heat vents, plug-ins, intercoms, television set). A classroom's barriers and openings are a rich and delightful exploratory concept for a class intent on understanding and designing their classroom's space.

Barriers. Walls and fences are not necessarily negative, and neither are the set of partitions (or barriers) that surround a classroom. They do define the class space and keep out unwanted things. Furthermore, they are fun to contemplate and decorate.

Just as our clothes and jewelry become decorative extensions of our personalities—communicating facets of ourselves to those who come upon us—so classroom walls and other partitions can also become an art gallery of sorts that reflects inwardly upon the inhabitants and helps them understand who they are and why they are there. Students might appropriately ask the following questions: Do our classroom partitions exhibit something in progress (creations) or only finished products (constructions)? Do the decorations ask questions or provide answers? Do they stagnate or continually change?

Displays on classroom walls and partitions can become a magic door that opens and psychologically sends students far beyond the classroom (such as pictures of foreign countries), or they can become a barrier door that closes and so shuts off questions, choices, and further exploration (such as posted classroom rules). They can also become a magic mirror that reflects back who the students are and what they might become (such as a display of student poetry).

Chalkboards and projector screens are transitory barriers, windows are transparent barriers, a shelf is a horizontal partition, clothing is a flexible moving partition, a drawer is a hidden barrier, and a ceiling is an interesting barrier to the sky that too few teachers and students explore.

Classroom objects can have multiple uses. For example, we can sit on a table and place something on the seat of a chair. We use a pencil to write on paper, but we can also use it to poke a hole in a sheet of paper, and a sheet of paper to make an origami bird.

Openings. Our brain's sensory and motor systems are our brain's in/out channels. What is their classroom equivalent? How do the variety of things that enter a classroom change before they leave?

We can make classroom things disappear without using a door or window: put something in a drawer, close the book, roll up the map, turn off the television, throw something in the wastebasket, close the drapes, erase the chalkboard, drink the water.

A walk around the neighborhood to observe the great variety in buildings, barriers, and openings can lead to interesting and imaginative observations and discussions about classroom space organization and utilization. Could a classroom contain the equivalent of a park? Could you increase classroom space through the imaginative use of floor, desk tops, shelves, and ceiling (effectively creating a multistory room)? Do rarely used objects need to occupy space that could be used for something frequently used? How many ways can the desks be arranged?

I learned something important about classroom space and myself during my final year as an elementary teacher. I was assigned to be one of the two sixth-grade teachers in a school. During the Labor Day weekend, I followed my custom of elaborately decorating my classroom for the first day of school. For example, I made displays that featured the science / social studies units I planned to teach that year. I developed a bulletin board display of my own sixth-grade year (pictures, events, magazine covers, etc.). I arranged floral displays. I even stuck golf tees into the ceiling's acoustic tile holes, and made an abstract ceiling design out of colored yarn that I looped around the tees. The room was truly impressively inviting.

The other sixth-grade teacher (who had not been on the staff the previous year) was not there that day, and so I looked into his room when I was done and was shocked to see a completely bare room—nothing on the walls or anywhere else. What a cold way to begin the year! I was concerned about our obviously different views of teaching and our potential collegial relationship, having had only a brief perfunctory opportunity to meet him at an off-campus pre-school event.

When school began the next day, my students were impressed with my work, and I spent the first hour or so describing the coming year through the various displays that I had developed.

By recess I was feeling quite good about myself and grim about my colleague. I walked next door and got the shock of my life. I discovered that when the school day began, my colleague had said in effect that they were all going to be together for a long time and that they would get to know him much sooner than he would get to know each of them (because 25 students observe only one teacher, and one teacher observes all 25 students). So their first assignment was to introduce themselves to him and to their classmates. "Spread yourself along a wall" was the way he put it.

What he had done before they arrived was to attach 30 numbered slips of paper on various room surfaces of different sizes and shapes—surface areas of windows, walls, chalkboards, file cabinets, doors, an area under a table, inside a drawer, and so forth. He asked students to select a numbered area that intrigued them and then sign their ownership of it on a numbered form on his desk.

He then brought out boxes of construction paper, magazines with lots of pictures, wallpaper samples, colored yarn, scissors, marking pens, and masking tape—everything a student might want in order to develop a display that would be an interesting self-advertisement.

The students obviously loved the assignment, and the room was glorious. The class was indeed spread across most of the room's surfaces. I slunk back into my room in chagrin, and confronted myself and my ego trip splattered all over my classroom. My ego was further reduced when my students asked after recess if we could all go next door to "see the really neat things that the other kids did."

I came to peace with myself over time. I felt that we were both good teachers who each developed a fine relationship with our students (and with each other). So our different approaches to the first day did not make or destroy the school year, and I certainly abandoned any sense of sole ownership of our classroom during the rest of the school year.

So it is okay to create an initial inviting environment that is the equivalent of the coming attraction clips in a film theater. Students do appreciate it when their teacher expends a lot of effort to initially interest them. It is also important to realize that it is not only the teacher's classroom but a room of shared ownership. My decorations were artfully crafted and elegant. The other classroom's decorations were funky, antic, personal, and, alas, also artfully crafted and elegant.

The following year, I went on to complete my graduate program, and so that was my final year as an elementary teacher. I thus did not have to decide what to do about my classroom at the beginning of the next year (and professors are transients in uniformly dreary university classrooms). Decades later, I am still not sure.

A socially stimulating environment will positively affect the physical development of our brain's cortex (Diamond & Hopson, 1998). The challenge is to determine how to create a socially stimulating classroom environment that gets as close as possible to the natural environment to which our brain is innately tuned. Such intriguing questions for a class to explore could include the following: At what decorating points does a classroom move from sterile to stimulating to cluttered? Do things that stimulate some students distract others? Which furniture configurations enhance, and which detract from social interaction? What is the appropriate relationship between the natural and electronic classroom environment at a time of increased influx of computer technology into the classroom (and into students' lives)? What about those few students who are uncomfortable in a classroom environment that the majority enjoy? This last question especially needs further exploration.

Cauliflower in the Classroom

Put a couple dozen people into a room for an extended period, and interpersonal problems related to space utilization will certainly develop. We use terms such as *protected space, territoriality, aggression*, and *predatory behavior* in the larger world, but comfortably shared space is also a genuine classroom management problem. Because it is sometimes easier to understand something by exploring it metaphorically, let us consider student space by imagining the plight of a plant.

Animals beset by predators have appendages that allow them to run, fly, or swim away from danger. Plants have roots that force them to remain where they are and suffer whatever indignities their predators intend, and many students feel similarly rooted to their desks, like plants. So how does a plant protect its personal space?

Over eons, plants have developed several successful defenses against predatory nibbling at their space (such as bark and hard coverings around their fruits). One intriguing plant defense seems to answer the question of why children tend to dislike the vegetables that they often later like as adults, and it also metaphorically suggests a cognitive explanation for some forms of student misbehavior.

Many plants (and especially wild plants) contain toxins, and the toxins differ from plant to plant (Nesse & Williams, 1994). The toxin levels are generally low enough so that they do not kill the animal, but nibbling herbivores will avoid that plant in the future if they find the taste obnoxious and digestion difficult. More commonly, animals diversify their diet to get all the nutrients they need, and so they limit their intake of any one toxin, and this, of course, is to the advantage of both plants and animals.

Toxin production uses plant resources and it can also be dangerous to the plant, so in general, plant tissues can have either a high level of toxins or rapid growth, but not both. Rapidly growing and easily replaced plant tissue such as leaves would thus have lower toxin levels than the more indispensable plant parts such as stems and roots. If you have to give up something to herbivores in the ecological battle, give them easily replaced leaves. Although we humans tend to eat a lot of leaves, we also eat the more toxic roots and stems (rather than the leaves) of some vegetables such as carrots, onions, asparagus, broccoli, and cauliflower.

Organisms differ in their susceptibility to toxins. Immature rapidly growing organisms are generally less able than mature organisms to tolerate toxins. Thus many children will consider the strong toxin-related odors and flavors of onions, broccoli, and similar vegetables to be obnoxious, whereas adults consider them spicy and somewhat pleasant.

Although children can often successfully (and perhaps honestly) complain to their parents about the bad taste of vegetables, an embryo has a more serious problem. Whatever the mother eats, the embryo eats, and a rapidly growing embryo is especially vulnerable to toxins. The embryonic solution apparently is to send a complaining chemical message to the mother that results in what we commonly call morning sickness. The result is that pregnant women are often nauseated by spicy foods and avoid them, to the benefit of the embryo. Profet (1992) reports that women who do not suffer from pregnancy nausea are more likely to miscarry or bear children with birth defects. (Similarly, pregnant women who use high levels of alcohol or other drugs risk Fetal Alcohol Syndrome and other disorders in their children.)

Even though parents historically did not actually know that some vegetables have low levels of toxicity that their children can detect, they have intuitively and often successfully used the responsive parental strategy of masking the sharp (toxin) flavors of vegetables in order to get their children to eat them, such as by placing sugar on carrots and cheese sauce on broccoli and cauliflower.

Whether that is a good thing is an interesting issue. Do children who most dislike such vegetables have a lower tolerance for the toxins than children who like vegetables? Can continually forcing children to eat something that nauseates them result in strong negative adult responses, such as the celebrated comment of former President George Bush that when he was a child he was forced to eat broccoli and he hated it and that as President of the United States he reveled in his power to refuse to serve broccoli in the White House? Should children be taught to put up with a little discomfort if the disliked food provides important nutrient values? Is student misbehavior thus a human equivalent to plant toxins?

Our common childhood negative response to vegetables has several interesting classroom parallels in instruction and management. Students similarly respond negatively to difficult-to-process school activities that focus on their bodybrain limitations.

1. *We are born with a brain that is genetically tuned to process such functions as respiration and circulation without any training.* Our brain is further tuned to the innate recognition of the normal sensory world—infants do not have to learn how to recognize line segments, tones, and smells (although they later have to learn their names). Young children need only limited help to effortlessly master such tasks as the local language and basic arithmetic functions. One reason why the mastery of reading and writing takes years of training and a lot of student effort when oral language was mastered effortlessly is that reading and writing emerged much later than oral language, only several thousand years ago, a relatively short time in terms of our brain's ability to evolve adaptations that combine abstract alphabet lines with speech sounds.

Basic arithmetic processes are similar. Infants can quickly determine such things as the quantity of up to about four items (such as that three items are more than two). Such simple quantity tasks are basic to our survival, so they are built into our cognitive system

(Dehaene, 1997). Advanced computational tasks came along later, and so they must be taught and are mastered with difficulty.

Because the motivation to master these more complex language and mathematical skills comes from the needs of our culture rather than from the natural innate problem-solving needs of a child's brain, we should not expect students to be any more pleased by school requirements to master such socially significant skills than they are to eat nutritious foods they do not like but that adults do, because in the adult view they are good for you.

Children are biologically focused on getting their motor system up to speed. They thus are not eager to spend 6 hours sitting at a desk in what they consider an uncomfortable environment and to exercise only their writing arm. Furthermore, asthmatic children who, for example, are allergic to cats or cigarette smoke are negatively affected by a classroom environment in which nearby students live with cats and smokers and so bring the allergens to school on their clothing.

2. *Our brain is organized so that our strengths often result in weakness in the opposite capability (as in handedness).* For example, our social wary brain has developed excellent conceptualization skills, the ability to rapidly size up and respond to value-laden situations. As indicated in Chapter 2, this survival strength requires a concomitant short attention span and a limited ability to track gradual change and to process details, because giving extended attention to anything would have made us vulnerable to such dangers as predatory animals creeping up from behind. To put it simply, our brain is not good at anything that requires solitary sustained attention and precision. Worksheets that require this tend to receive the same grousing that cauliflower and broccoli receive at dinner. Our brain has a low tolerance for tasks and settings that natural selection has yet to deem important.

Students tend to respond happily to activities that their brains developed to do well such as exploring concepts, discovering patterns, estimating and predicting, cooperating on group projects, and discussing moral/ethical issues. Conversely, classroom misbehavior tends to emerge out of factually driven memorizing assignments that require solitary sustained effort and precision.

We tend to sugarcoat such activities, just as we sugar the carrots to make them palatable. We play multiplication tables relay games, run spelling bees, and give prizes for high achievement, all to get students' minds off their cognitive weaknesses, to pretend that such learning does not need to come with effort. A concern we will have to confront is whether making something enjoyable in school is always a good idea. Would we be better off to simply level with students that some culturally important cognitive capabilities require conscious effort and practice to develop?

Conversely, forcing students to spend their days in an uncomfortable classroom environment to master information and skills they do not consider relevant can result in a lifelong aversion to history, math, or whatever. The adult George Bush is intelligent enough to realize that broccoli would enhance his diet, but he still dislikes it.

Biologically protective defenses (such as those of cauliflower) suggest that personal territoriality and its protection are important concerns when we attempt to design a single comfortable classroom environment for an entire group that is made up of individuals. To develop democratic values in a class means that the minority must accept the will of the majority (which is what legislation and elections are about) but also that the majority must respect the individual rights of the minority (which is what the courts are about). Classroom space utilization is not an easy issue for a class (and a teacher with veto power) to democratically work out, just as it is difficult for cities and states to develop acceptable land use regulations. But teacher and students should realize that it can be a very important exploration because students who can discover how best to share classroom space will become adult citizens who will know how to share political space.

Consider the plight and probable destiny of a dandelion plant in the middle of a bright green lawn. It has a beautiful yellow flower, and the plant itself can be used in salads and to make wine. Children love to blow off and so spread its ball of hundreds of seeds. What more could one want of a simple plant than beauty, food, wine, and entertainment? But we homeowners typically consider it a weed that must be eradicated because we want the lawn to be uniformly green. We tend to believe that colorful flowers (and only hybrids, please) belong in the flower bed next to the green lawn. It is the botanical equivalent of the racist, sexist, elitist, and so forth view that "you don't belong here if I didn't select you."

This is why helping students discover the shared dynamics of classroom space is an important continuing part of classroom management. The activities suggested throughout this chapter and in the section that follows should initially help students to simply become more aware of space, and especially the space the group occupies, and this enhanced awareness should lead to the genuinely shared appropriate and imaginative use of school space.

Suggested Activities

A Special Place

Young people today spend a lot of time carefully observing the 1-square-foot, remarkable brightly colored, rapidly fluctuating, electronic worlds of television, video games, and computers. Video game success requires an intense functional knowledge of seen and unseen electronic objects that flit about the screen. Surfing the Internet requires the ability to simultaneously manipulate a wide variety of electronic environments, only one of which is immediately visible.

The natural biological world that students also inhabit has its own slower rhythms, and young people should also carefully explore it. The following activity does. Introduce it and see how far you can take it. Do not worry that not everyone will get into the spirit of the activity and stay with it. Allow it to evolve over time with those who tune into it.

Ask each student to identify an exploratory space in the natural world that is about the size of a television screen, and then to regularly observe it. Possibilities include a marked-off home garden or lawn area, an aquarium, and an ant nest. It is also okay to go beyond such limitations and observe such things as a family pet or baby sibling, the view out a bedroom window, an outdoor shrub or indoor plant, a seat in a nearby mall, a set of backyard squirrels, or whatever seems interesting.

Ask students to set up a regular 15-minute period to quietly observe the site and record what occurs. It could be a daily observation, or one done only several times a week, but it is important to keep a regular schedule that a student can easily remember and maintain.

Ask students to develop a journal to record their observations, a page for each 15-minute period (typing observations into a computer file is okay, but it somehow seems curiously out of the spirit of the activity). The observation episodes will initially tend to focus on measurements such as how many leaves does the plant have, how many people walked by the mall bench, and how many insects visited the area. Students will create maps that trace the paths of the crawling infant, the family pet, the aquarium fish, and sketch pictures of organisms in the area.

Students will soon move toward more subtle observations such as noting changes that occurred between observation episodes, wondering about things that have disappeared, and making predictions of what might occur. Magnifying glasses, tape recorders, and cameras emerge as students dig deeper into and improve their understanding of their small segment of the biological world.

As the project continues, ask students to report on interesting things they have discovered and encourage all in the class to seek parallels between (a) their microworlds and the larger world (and especially their classroom) and (b) the electronic world they are also exploring daily.

Preparatory Activities

What follows are some activities that you might use as a lead-up to the "Special Place" project described above. Much of the passing scene fortunately bypasses our conscious attention. Imagine the cognitive overload if we were consciously aware of everything in our environment. Still, we often ignore things we should consciously attend to, and so the following activities will lead to interesting discussions about what we tend to notice and do not notice in our environment.

1. Ask your students to recall and then sketch what is on a currently nonvisible school wall they see daily (the school entrance, a cafeteria wall, etc.). Then ask them to look only toward the front of the classroom and sketch what is on the wall behind them. Quietly ask a student to temporarily leave the room and then ask the class to write descriptions of the student's outer clothing (type of garment, color, etc.). Ask your students to draw two large circles on a sheet of paper and sketch (or use words and arrows to identify and locate) the four elements on each side of a penny (a coin they handle

frequently). Tabulate, graph, and discuss the results of such tests. For example, why did some students do better than others, and why did students do better on some tests than others?

2. Speech allows us to create sound representations of visual phenomena—which can be helpful during a telephone conversation—but words often cannot easily convey what our visual system sees. Place a common object such as scissors, a comb, or a sock in a box so students cannot see it. Ask a student to look in the box and use less than a minute to describe the object, without naming it or indicating its use. Ask the rest to write what they think it is and discuss the results. What descriptive words/phrases helped the most, the least? Repeat the activity several times with different describers and objects to see if the descriptions and scores improve over time. Use this activity to help prepare your students for the journal they will keep in the "Special Place" project.

3. We use all our senses to orient ourselves in space, and so it is interesting to reduce the sensory information and discover if students can still identify something. Tape-record several common school sounds (such as a flushing toilet, the push bar on the front door, a drinking fountain, a playground swing, or the sounds in the office, cafeteria, gym). Play the tape to discover how many students can identify and/or locate the sound. Do the same thing with smell by placing objects with distinctive odors (such as the school soap, a piece of some of today's lunch, crayons, chalk) in opaque glass containers with holes punched into the lid. Ask students to sniff and identify. Shoot slides of a small segment of a variety of large school areas (such as part of the front door, the classroom ceiling, the cafeteria counter, the side of a school bus). Show the slides and ask students to identify the space. Use these activities to encourage multisensory observations in the "Special Place" project.

4. Color plays an important role in our perception of space. If the classroom has a window that the sun shines through, paste various colored cellophane shapes on the window and note the moving colored patterns that move across the room during the day. Bring some light fixtures to school and place different colored light bulbs in them. String colored Christmas lights. Place several colored slips of paper in a box and take one out each Friday before dismissal. See how much of that color you and your students can introduce into the room during the next week. Suppose you drew a blue slip

on Friday. Display pictures in which blues dominate, get some plants with blue flowers, feature blue in bulletin board displays, and encourage students to wear blue clothing (and line them up from the lightest to darkest blue).

Chapter ❺

Spending, Saving, and Using Time

●———————————————————●

Time is an elusive concept that we tend to view as a cultural commodity. We spend, save, and use time. We consider it precious but often waste it. Children earn free time, and are punished with time-out. We are early, late, or on time. Time flies and drags as it moves us from the past to the present and into future. We are having the time of our life. Our time is up. In short, time is nature's way of keeping everything from happening all at once.

Our brain oddly has no specific system to recognize and regulate time, even though we function within a large number of important cycles, rhythms, and sequences, such as those that regulate sleeping and waking, feelings of hunger and satiation, and sex hormone distribution. We can experience time as being discrete (a series of specific events) or as continuous (a sequence of events that flow together into something we will later recall simply as a *party*). Time can exist as an objective chronological sequence of clock ticks and calendar dates, or it can be subjectively flexible (how long it seems to take for a red light to change, or a boring activity to end). We tend to automatically wake up at about the same time every morning, and many people awaken briefly from a dream at approximately 3 a.m. School time is about schedules, lesson lengths, grade sequences, due dates, waiting, and much more.

Three of Gardner's (1998) nine forms of intelligence focus on time and sequence: linguistic, musical, and logical-mathematical intelligences. How are these related to time/sequence? All exploit a marvelous biological principle that allows an organism to use a small number of discrete coding elements to pack an incredible amount of complex information units into a limited biological space: Code the information into the sequence of a relatively small number of separate elements and the length of the coding chain rather than into the elements themselves.

To revisit and expand the discussion in Chapter 1, we have created an English language of 500,000 words out of 26 letters (or 45 phonemes) by inserting the meaning of a word into its letter sequence and length rather than into the individual letters themselves (such as with *do, dog, god, good,* and *goods*). We can similarly create an infinite number of melodies out of various sequences of the 12 tones in the musical scale, and a very complex numerical/mathematical system out of 10 digits (321 not being the same as 123). Imagine the huge amount of brain space we would need to store and process our complex language, music, and mathematical systems without this efficient coding system.

We can further string words into a sentence and sentences into a paragraph, and a sequence of events into a story (and storytelling in its various forms occupies much of our life). Logical thought processes tend to focus on what we will do first, second, third, and so on, and why we will follow that particular sequence.

It is intriguing (and somewhat mystical) that the genetic coding system of all organisms also functions similarly, sequentially. The nucleus of every cell in our body contains a yard-long, 50 trillionths of an inch wide, ladder-shaped, deeply-folded, identical string of deoxyribonucleic acid (DNA), the recipe book for manufacturing cellular materials and regulating cellular processes. Twenty amino acids constitute the ingredients for all plant and animal protein synthesis, and the DNA sequence of a gene (the recipe for constructing a protein) is the sequence of amino acids and the length of the amino acid chain that creates the protein. So we use several sequential language coding systems to communicate within one generation, and a similarly organized genetic coding sequence to create and maintain the children who will become the next generation.

How to appropriately manage the sequence of events that we experience as time is thus an important human challenge, so teachers and students should seek to understand and explore time and its various dynamics in both classroom and life management.

This chapter introduces and discusses three human time/ sequence concepts that have rich exploratory possibilities for a creative class interested in the concept of classroom time management: (a) life span, and especially the first two decades of life, (b) time allocations during a school year, and (c) time allocations during an average preadult day.

Life Span: Two Developmental Decades

A key element of the concept of a life span is that we are a dependent social species, quite helpless at birth, with a brain one third its adult size. Our approximately 20-year developmental trajectory includes a very dependent childhood decade during which our parents and other adults provide an important protective barrier and needed instruction while our bodybrain systems come on line, and a less protected adolescence decade during which the systems mature to the generally effective level of adult life.

Adult life signals a role shift as we become the caretakers of the next generation of dependent children through the direct challenge of parenthood and/or the more indirect challenge of paying taxes and contributing to charities to help support dependent citizens. Finally, adults who live long enough often revert back to a dependent status through family and governmental support systems.

Childhood

During the years from birth to age 10, our developmental focus is on learning how to be a human being: learning to move, to communicate, to master basic social skills. These often require the mastery of learned social and cultural conventions, traditions, and rituals (such as the mastery of movements associated with various games, of the differences in various spoken and written languages, and of our culture's definition of good manners).

The initial development of these abilities is slow and awkward, but children are generally able to function at a rapid automatic (reflexive) level by the age of 10. Adults generally allow young children to make many mistakes as they stumble toward the mastery of basic human skills and knowledge. We smile indulgently and offer support rather than criticism as toddlers trip and 2-year-olds make language errors. We are there principally to protect their safety and to applaud their successes because we realize that toddling leads to walking and running, and babbling leads to smooth speaking, reading, and writing. It is developmental speed-up time, but we are typically in no hurry.

The situation is similar with the initially awkward development of social skills. Children tend to closely observe and model the social behavior of their parents and other adults. School further provides them with a marvelous laboratory for social learning and exploration, from structured magic circles to free-flowing recess behavior. Their fellow explorers are peers from families espousing a variety of values, and they all have to learn how to get along in an institutional setting that differs considerably from the informality of home. Student misbehavior can thus become an important diagnostic part of the social curriculum (much as pain is the first step to physical healing).

The school social environment should be challenging but not too threatening to children who are learning how to negotiate their way through the real social problems they confront. It certainly helps if the family and neighborhood also enhance a student's personal and social development, but schools must work with whoever comes through the door, at whatever their developmental level, with whatever problems they have. The goal is to help move children to an almost automatic expression of basic social skills (such as occurs with their basic language and math skills).

Our current obsession with raising academic standards has led to a diminished focus on school time devoted to the basics of personal and social development and conflict resolution, and to a reduction in specialized staff trained to identify and counsel those with a potential for destructive and other forms of antisocial behavior. The recent series of secondary school killings argues for a reexamination of such decisions. The movement of the socially inept to deviant social groups often begins during the elementary school years.

The best long-term strategy for reducing antisocial behavior is probably to identify young children who are at risk and to place them into intervention programs that will help them develop the social skills and coping strategies they need. The First Step to Success program (Walker, 1998), for example, begins in kindergarten.

Self-contained classrooms are common in elementary schools, and they provide a better environment than departmentalized schools for exploring time. Bells do not ring with 43-minute regularity, so activities can be stretched out or compressed. Certain activities, such as going to the library, physical education, and lunch are scheduled, but there is still a lot of exploratory flexibility about the scheduling, length, and spacing of activities. For example, what is best first off, and what is best at the end of the day? Should sedentary activities be followed by movement, individual-by-group activities? Are Monday and Friday different kinds of days than Tuesday through Thursday? Find out by exploring ideas with your class, trying out different ways to schedule the day and gathering data on what you do.

Adolescence

From ages 10 to 20, we focus on learning how to be a productive, reproductive human being, planning for a vocation and exploring emotional commitment and sexuality. The early part of this period is incredibly challenging.

We go through seven profound biological changes during our life, and three of these generally occur between the ages of 10 and 14 (the middle school years)! The seven changes include birth and death, the mid- to late-life lessening of our reproductive and cognitive capabilities, and the following three major early adolescent shifts:

- From childhood to puberty, the onset of our reproductive capabilities
- From concrete to formal operations, the (Piagetian) maturation of intelligence
- From an authoritarian to a consensus morality, the maturation of our personal and social identity

The timely adolescent maturation of our brain's frontal lobes is central to the success of all three developmental shifts. The frontal lobes play key roles in attention, reflective thought, and problem solving. Highly interconnected with our subcortical, more reflexive processing systems, they can inhibit impulsive and inappropriate behavior.

We could consider the years from ages 10 through 20 as a second childhood, the awkward beginnings in each of the three major areas of change, the gradual movement toward the confidence and competence characterized by upper adolescent frontal-lobe-driven response patterns that are often delayed and reflective (rather than rapid and reflexive).

Busy as adolescents often are, their lives actually slow down somewhat. They hang out, often not doing much of anything. They daydream. Music becomes central to their lives because song slows down speech so we can insert melody, harmony, rhythm, and volume into the long but simple musically emotional messages of love and hate and of commitment and alienation that we use to slowly explore our emerging personal and social relationships. The music of our adolescence helps define our personal and social identity even though adults have seemingly always tended to scorn the music their children create and embrace (my parents thought that Glenn Miller's music was sensuously destructive).

Unfortunately, adults frequently do not offer early adolescents the same warm indulgence and social protection that they provided a decade earlier. We appreciated their preadolescent move toward rapid, reflexive, correct responses, and so we now want them to quickly get their act together (oblivious of the reality that many 40-year-olds are still struggling with their sexuality and morality). We respond to the adolescent awkward explorations of sexuality, critical thinking, and identity with a tendency to deride their initial simplistic solutions to complex problems, and we are leery of their early romantic friendships and shifts from our family's values.

Adolescents sense this and typically attempt to distance themselves from the adults who offered them such unconditional nurturing a decade earlier. Adolescents tend to affect clothing, adornment, and behavior styles they know will displease adults. They now seek the advice and nurturing, which their parents had once provided from their peers, through introspection, and alas, from trashy mass media examples of aggressively inept conflict resolution. Those who did not develop effective social skills during their first decade must now seek friendships from within a smaller pool of peers, generally those who are similarly rejected by the socially successful. The socially competent will generally support each other because we are a cooperative social species, but we cooperate with those in our perceived group, and we tend to be wary of others, often expressing it in speech and manner. The adolescent alienation of the rejected increases.

Puberty signals the biological capacity for adult relationships and parenthood, and so this parental and family distancing is actually developmentally important. We cannot maintain our primary allegiance to our childhood family while simultaneously beginning the process of forming our own mature relationships. For example, spousal relationships tend to diminish if one partner is too psychologically tied to his or her childhood family and/or friends.

Unfortunately, our biological readiness for parenthood occurs a decade or so before most adolescents are culturally ready for such commitment. Thus, many disassociate from their family in their search for a personal identity, with no bonding alternative in sight. Adolescent organizations and informal social groupings fill the void for many, and provide a useful vehicle for developing and rehearsing positive social skills. In a secondary school culture of cliques, however, the socially rejected become even more alienated from peers who could possibly help them if any positive connection could develop. Such negative alliances as troubled couples and adolescent gangs are one unfortunate (but psychologically understandable) solution to this alienation.

Secondary schools tend to be departmentalized and are often more concerned with the successful mastery of subjects. Because secondary schools are typically more beset by political pressures to excel, they are more oriented toward increasing the pressure on students during a decade in which adolescents need to slow down, consolidate the explosive motor and social development of their first decade, and discover themselves. Elementary school class explorations of how best to understand and use class time seem an impossible luxury to secondary school teachers, and yet it is equally necessary to explore adolescent time.

For example, at puberty, many young people go through a period of continual jet lag. They seem now to live a couple time zones west from where they actually are, going to bed and awakening later than formerly. It is related to the hormonal changes young people go through at puberty. We have always known about it (even if we did not understand it), but the secondary school buses and school schedule run as if all adolescents are wide awake by

8 a.m. The result, as any secondary school teacher knows, is that the first periods are a drowsy disaster for many students. Any hope for a creative solution?

Perhaps. We are approaching a time when schools will have much more access to computer technology. The secondary school curriculum is composed of elements that are either (a) personally directed and can thus be processed and mastered individually through the use of computer software or (b) best mastered through the social interaction of students in a classroom.

One could therefore imagine a future secondary school schedule that would focus on individual computer-driven studies from (perhaps) 8 to 10 a.m. and 3 to 5 p.m., and focus on the socially interactive curricula from 10 a.m. to 3 p.m. Students would attend from 8 a.m. to 3 p.m., or from 10 a.m. to 5 p.m. (depending on their sleep/waking cycle or other commitments). The school would need enough individual computer technology for half the student body in the early and late segments, and enough classroom space to accommodate all students during the midday block when all are present. Existing schools typically have that spatial capability. Staff schedules could be shifted to accommodate the longer day so that students would have at least periodic individual access to their teachers (as needed) during the individually oriented blocks at the beginning and end of the day.

Despite all sorts of problems with bus schedules, sports, teacher schedules, staff meetings, the availability of useful software, and whatever other problems folks will suggest, it is not an impossible scenario. But nothing will ever change unless educators begin to imagine that there might be a better way to organize time in an adolescent student's life and then seek creative solutions.

A Year's Curricular Time

We can separate the division of time in our personal lives and the school curriculum into three categories of activity that are driven by internal and external forces. Some of our lifetime is prescribed by societal needs such as to be a productive citizen, and so our job demands our attendance during certain time blocks. Some of our time is prescribed by human conditions such as to care for our own bodily needs and to come to the aid of an injured person. Some of our time also is devoted to personal interests such as hobbies, mass media, and recreation.

We differ much in our allocation of time to these three categories. Some people must work long hours at a low-paying job to merely survive, and so personal needs and interests get limited time. Others are retired or independently wealthy, and so they may spend most of their time on such things as personal interests, body care, and charitable endeavors.

A school year has about 1,000 hours. We can divide curricular time into the same three categories and raise the issue of the appropriate allocation of time among the three.

The Formal Curriculum

Most people consider the term *curriculum* to be related to such concepts as required courses and programs, scope and sequence issues, and state standards. The formal curriculum represents society's concern for prescribed minimum mastery standards in selected socially important subject areas and the belief that instruction should proceed in a systematic fashion. Most of the instructional and materials budget is spent on this part of the curriculum.

The language arts, in their various forms, dominate this part of the elementary curriculum. Furthermore, vocabulary development (learning the names of things) is a major focus of most other elementary curricular areas such as science and social studies. The secondary school curriculum is a mix of required and elective courses with the total number and focus of academic units being what is formally prescribed. Large schools tend to have a richer assortment of elective courses.

The formal curriculum is important in that it develops standardization and balance in a school system in which students transfer among schools, but it can become a negative force if it so dominates the program that educators and patrons ignore other important elements in the education of young people. The negative human-time equivalent of this limited perspective would be workaholics, those who are so psychologically tied to the perceived demands of their job that they do not know what to do and cannot relax at home, on vacations, and upon retirement.

The Responsive Curriculum

This part of the curriculum focuses on (often unpredictable) events that intrude into the curriculum because of their immediate noteworthiness (e.g., a war, a storm, a community celebration, a house being moved down the street). These events are prescribed in that it is almost impossible to ignore them, even though they might not easily fit into the current curriculum. In nonschool terms, it is like a car accident intruding on an already busy day. One simply has to reschedule things and respond to the importance and immediacy of the accident.

Curricular guides and materials for unpredictable developments are typically nonexistent. Teachers tend to create something on the fly as the events unfold. I was a sixth-grade teacher on Saturday, October 5, 1957, when the world's first satellite (Sputnik) went into orbit. The Russians had made no previous announcement of their intentions.

I realized when the event was reported on the evening news that it would become a major historical event in my students' lives, and so I decided to focus on it on Monday despite my general lack of knowledge of the topic. I went to the library to learn as much as possible, and I checked the district's AV catalog for any useful materials. I (and many other teachers, I am sure) initiated a study of rockets and satellites on Monday. I told my students that we would have to be co-learners in the enterprise because my knowledge was limited. They were delighted to discover an important topic that they knew as much about as their teacher (practically nothing), and so we collaborated on designing an investigation that went on for several weeks (and intruded seriously into the formal curriculum). We ended our study by making and launching rockets. Many classes do rocket launches now, but it is much more exciting to do something like this at the point of the historical event. I have chanced upon several students in that class over the years, and most told me without prompting that our satellite study was the most memorable event of their elementary school years.

The assassinations of President Kennedy and Martin Luther King, the *Challenger* explosion (observed on classroom television by many students because a teacher was aboard), the eruption of Mt. St. Helens, the Clinton impeachment trial, and the recent series of high school murders are other examples of major unpredictable historical events that teachers have had to respond to at one level or another.

Teachers sometimes know about an important coming event that does not easily fit into the current formal curriculum—such as a presidential election, a community centennial celebration, or the first moon landing—and can prepare for it. Mass media and the Internet are generally a rich source of information for such curricular investigations.

Certain classes of events are unpredictable but have a high probability of occurring during the course of the year, and so teachers often determine in advance how they will handle such situations when they occur. A death, storm damage, and the closing of a company that employs the parents of many students are examples.

One problem with this part of the curriculum is that teachers get limited guidance for how to deal with such problem situations, and the immediacy of the event can lead to an inappropriate response. A young woman told me that her father died in an accident when she was in the fourth grade, and so she missed a week of school. Her teacher told her classmates before her return to avoid comments and questions about the death—the less said the better. A dozen years later she was still deeply grieved that her father had lived a loving and productive life, and when he died, neither his life nor his death was mentioned in her classroom by a teacher and classmates who, she now realizes, incorrectly thought they were being kind to her.

The Informal Curriculum

This segment of the curriculum focuses on cultural areas of special interest to teachers and/or students. They arise out of avocations, hobbies, the nature of the class, the availability of materials, and the location of the school. They are neither required nor prohibited by the school. They get into the curriculum because people enjoy doing them, and so they add a pinch of spice to the curriculum. I have known many teachers who insert their personal interests and hobbies into the curriculum.

I was interested in the Japanese art of origami (paper folding), and so I always taught it to my elementary school students. No one said I should, and no one said I should not. My students enjoyed it in part because they discovered a little bit of me and my interests in the process, and origami is an intriguing challenge.

Conversely, a fifth-grade teacher I once met had an extensive mineral collection and knew a lot about geology. When I asked him how he incorporated his knowledge and collection into his teaching, he told me that he did not mention it to his students, let alone teach it. He said that in his previous school, students were always bringing rocks to him to identify. It finally irritated him, and so he decided to keep his hobby to himself at his current school. How absolutely sad!

Every class has students with knowledge that should be tapped. Years later, I can still recall a budding fourth-grade ornithologist who did most of the teaching in a science unit on birds, a fifth grader who proudly took us on a field trip through his parents' paint business, a seventh grader who taught us all to weave, and a sixth grader who taught us how to compose songs. This informal part of the curriculum gets to the heart of primary grade show-and-tell time, elementary school interest groups, secondary school electives, and extracurricular programs.

I have always found the discussion interesting when a group of educators tries to determine how time should properly be apportioned among these three categories of curricular time. Ask a group of teachers to individually jot down percentages that indicate approximately (a) how much time they currently devote to each category across the year and then (b) how they would prefer to allocate the 100% among the three categories. Tabulate and graph the results. What factors might affect the allocations (grade level, years of experience, gender)? It is interesting for teachers to hear their colleagues explain their allocations and the differences between their practice and preference.

Informal surveys discovered that inexperienced teachers tended to focus on the formal curriculum. This is not surprising because they are concerned with their continued employment and so realize they must do well with district programs that they are still trying to understand. We also found that teachers with many years of experience who seemed to be suffering from burnout focused more on the formal curriculum, and this also is not surprising. It is what a teacher can typically teach with the least effort.

Teachers who seemed a cut above the norm tended to focus more on the responsive curriculum. Their comments suggested that they were aware of educationally significant events that occurred in the community and beyond, and they inserted such events into the curriculum, often finding ways to insert these events into the formal curriculum or encourage interested students to explore them through informal investigations.

> This time allocation is also a good issue for an elementary or secondary class to explore. Introduce the issue by asking them to keep a log for several days indicating how they apportioned their personal time across the three categories (societal demands, body needs, and personal interests). Then keep records on how class time was allocated across the categories for a couple weeks. The study should lead to discussions and explorations of different curricular time allocations.

A Day in the Life

We live through about 150,000 hours between the ages of 1 and 18. We sleep about 50,000 hours of this time, and we dream about 2 hours of the 8 hours we sleep each night. Sleeping and dreaming appear to be positively related to the development and maintenance of the long-term memories that emerge out of daytime activities because they allow our brain to eliminate the interference of sensorimotor activity while it physically adds to, edits, and erases the neural network connections that create long-term memories.

We spend about 65,000 of our 100,000 waking hours involved in solitary activities and in direct, informal value-laden relationships with family and friends, activities that play a major role in the development and maintenance of important personal memories and interests.

We spend about 35,000 of our waking hours with our larger culture in formal and informal metaphoric-symbolic activities: about 12,000 hours in school, and about twice that much with the various forms of mass media (such as television, computers, films, music, sports, nonschool print media, churches, and museums). Mass media and the school thus play major roles in the development and maintenance of important cultural memories and skills.

So on an average developmental day between the ages of 1 and 18, a young person sleeps 8 hours and spends 10 waking hours with self, family, and friends; 4 hours with mass media; and only 2 hours in school. Our society has incredible expectations for those 2 hours!

We can think of the family as a vertically organized social system composed of people of various ages who live together. The parental older members typically control the resources, and they do what they can to inculcate their values into the younger members. Parents are thus much interested in promoting their personal view of the concepts of right and wrong.

A K-12 classroom is a horizontally organized social system composed of a group of young people of about the same age (and one older official representative of adult society). The students come from separate (vertically organized) families that may differ substantially in their values on many issues. Schools thus focus mostly on the less controversial concepts of true and false—factual information and skills with high community agreement (such as that $6 \times 5 = 30$, c-a-t spells *cat*, and Washington, DC is the capital of the United States). Schools have historically avoided controversial (right/wrong) cultural issues, such as issues related to religious beliefs, sexual practices, and politics. Schools may explain the expressed (true/false) differences among political parties on a given issue but will not presume to indicate which position is right or wrong.

It is actually difficult to identify any cultural value that enjoys total community agreement. Even the seemingly straightforward injunction to not kill people is fraught with disagreement when one considers such value-laden cultural practices as abortion, capital punishment, war, mercy killing, industrial pollution, and assisted suicide.

Classroom management policies and practices obviously involve value judgments, from attention to bad manners, crude language, dress, and beyond. It is one thing to create school behavioral boundaries and another thing to say (for example) that certain expressions are inherently crude (when a student's parents may commonly use the terms at home). Almost everything that occurs in school is value laden at one level or another, but educators try to distinguish between a value decision the school made to maintain order and the absolute rightness of that decision. Classroom management thus involves a lot of negotiating among educators, students, and parents. Chapter 7 revisits this issue.

Behavioral evaluation is a difficult issue. Public schools must initially accept the values of entering students and their families (if their values are not immoral or illegal), even though the student may be somewhat troublesome. The school begins where the students are and works toward eventual student acceptance of school behavioral expectations. It is curious that parents, who are often so insistent about periodic precise evaluations of their children's school development, do not grade their home behavior even though they have much more personal access to their children's behavior than the school does. The reasoning perhaps is that family values generally develop through an extended period of negotiation between parents and child, and it is difficult for parents to know the strength of the family values at any given time (and one could argue that it is equally difficult to precisely know the academic developmental level of much that parents expect the school to precisely assess).

It is important to realize that many agencies other than the family and school play key enculturation roles during childhood and adolescence. Electronic mass media has especially emerged recently to considerably broaden children's access to the world. What occurs anywhere is now known everywhere. Mass media provide a curious mix of information and values. The credibility of the information varies tremendously, and impressionable young people often lack the ability to differentiate sense from nonsense in mass media.

Although the family controls (or ought to control) a child's access to these other enculturation agencies, students typically bring a wide range of information and values from such agencies into a classroom's curriculum. Even though the school has no control over the information children gather during nonschool time, parents may become distressed when such information gets inserted into a class discussion.

Chapter 3 posed the issue of the appropriate control of a classroom year. It suggested that one could metaphorically think (a) of an externally controlled protected environment (akin to that of a fetus in a womb) in which the school would control curricular content and events, or (b) of a more self-controlled exploratory environment (akin to that of a person's life) quite open to the extended exploration of a wide range of information and values.

Although school actually occupies a relatively small part of a child's first two decades, it does get prime time, and the students generally do not have a remote control to change the channel if they do not like the current curriculum (as they sometimes do with mass media and other nonschool activities). School time is thus important time in a student's life, even though its focus generally differs from personal, family, peer, and mass media time. School provides access to information and skills that are rarely the focus of these other educative agencies. It is organized to enhance social awareness and skills. It often moves a student beyond immediate family values and traditions into contacts with other ways of thinking about and doing things.

This chapter began with the suggestion that our culture tends to think of time as a commodity, and so a continuing challenge to educators is to spend school time wisely, despite a lack of clear consensus on how that might be done.

Suggested Activities

Students tend to experience each school day for what it is, and to not notice the gradual sweep of time over the school year. The following activities provide them with a sense of that.

A Room Diary

This year-long activity works best in an elementary self-contained classroom or middle school homeroom. Schedule the students so that one student is assigned each day to be the room reporter (and to not participate directly in class activities and assignments). Locate the reporter at a separate table with a good view of the entire room (to facilitate the observation and recording of formal and informal events). It is also a good idea to ask the student to take one picture (on a Polaroid camera) of the event that best photographically characterized the day. Toward the end of the day, ask the student to summarize his or her observations on a one-page narrative report of what occurred that was interesting and memorable, and to read it to the class just before dismissal.

Ask the student to type the report into a wordprocessor form (that allows space to scan the picture onto the page, if you include a photograph in this diary activity). It is also useful to include such information as attendance and weather into each day's report. Print a copy of the day's report and place it into a three-ring binder.

The next person on the list becomes the reporter the next day. Over the course of the year, each student will be the reporter about six times. Students will read the diary frequently during the year, and it will become a useful reference about events and decisions. It is obviously important at the beginning of the year to instruct them in how to observe, record, and summarize a day and to caution them against hurtful comments (humor is great, ridicule is not).

The marvelous thing about this activity is that at the end of the year you can duplicate a copy of the room diary (perhaps 180 pages) for each student. Teach a bookbinding unit toward the end of the year, and each student will leave with a complete personally bound record of the year. If the duplicating/binding cost per diary (under $5) creates a problem, encourage your class to explore creative fund-raising activities.

A Headline Diary

Cut out the lead page headline of the local paper each day of the school year and, starting at the top, paste the headlines in sequence on a sheet of butcher paper. Newspaper pages are usually about a foot wide, and the lead headline is about an inch high. It would thus require about a 1 by 3-foot sheet of paper to record the major event of each day during a month. Post them all at the end of the school year and discuss the events that the students most remember.

A Vine Line

Use a fast-growing vine (such as ivy) to record important events across the year. Plant it into a pot in one corner of the room, continually remove lateral growth, train it up the wall so it is above the chalkboard, and then allow it to grow horizontally along the top of the chalkboard and beyond, as far around the room as it can move over the course of the year.

Attach identifying index cards to the wall and place an arrow at the point where the tip of the vine is on specific days during the year (such as Halloween, students' birthdays). It is also fun for students to predict (a month or so in advance) where the vine tip might be on their birthday.

Birthdays

About a week or so before their birthdays, ask students to go to the public library and use newspapers and magazines to discover what important events occurred in the community and world on the day they were born (or shortly before and after). Their parents may also be able to provide such information (although some parents are so concerned with the birth that the rest of the world does not really register that day). Ask students to report their discoveries on the school day closest to their birthday. It is important for your students to begin to develop a sense of the relationship between their lifetime and world history.

On a personal note, I have always been fascinated that Charles Lindbergh flew across the Atlantic 3 months after I was born, that DNA was discovered 4 years after I graduated from college with a degree in biology, and that the computer chip was developed shortly before I joined the University of Oregon faculty. Thus commercial flight developed during my lifetime, biology and medicine matured during my professional life, and the computer revolution occurred during my last job!

Wait Time

Wait time is the amount of time that teachers will wait after asking a question before they ask another student or answer it themselves. It actually averages around 3 seconds, and the better students usually get more time to respond than the poorer students. You can check yourself by giving a student a stopwatch, and asking him or her to record your behavior during a lesson, the length of the series of intervals between a question you ask and when you speak again if no student response is forthcoming. You may discover that although we seek reflective thought in the classroom we often encourage a reflexive rhythm.

Chapter 6

Managing Movement

M ovement is a manifestation of life itself. Even in seeming stillness, our body teems with movement: the beat of our heart, the contractions and expansions of our lungs, the movement of digesting food, neural impulses coursing through our brain, and viral and bacterial invaders moving about. To be perfectly still is to be perfectly dead.

Chapter 2 suggested that mobility provides us with the central reason for a brain. Plants seem to do fine without one, with many trees far outliving us. We have a brain because we have leg, arm, and head muscle systems that allow us to move toward opportunities and away from danger. Plants must stay and take whatever comes along, including predators that nibble leaves and commit other indignities (toxins and bark providing limited protection, as suggested in Chapter 4). Why would an immobile tree even want a sensory system that could recognize an approaching logger?

Consider the sea squirt, which initially has a brain and swims about until it finds a place with sufficient nutrients. It then permanently attaches to a nearby rock or coral and begins the rest of its immobile life by eating its now superfluous brain.

Because we humans move throughout life, we need an intelligent cognitive system that can transform sensory input and imagination into appropriate motor output; to decide what is good and bad about here and there, and then to move or stay. Mobility is thus central to much that is human, whether the movement of information is physical or psychological (such as running toward or speaking to someone). We can move and talk, trees cannot. Misguided teachers who constantly tell their students to sit down and be quiet imply a preference for working with a grove of trees and not a classroom of students.

This book focuses principally on energy, space, time, movement, and range as they relate to the management of life and classrooms. When we expend energy in our space/time world, movement within biological and cultural ranges generally occurs. Movement thus combines energy, space, and time within limits.

It is also probably safe to say that most classroom misbehavior involves the movement of people, objects, or sounds—running, slouching, hitting, throwing things, being noisy, using vulgar language, and so forth. Many disciplinary measures also involve movement (or nonmovement) such as a verbal reprimand, movement toward the misbehaving student, a request to sit down, an office referral, or detention.

This chapter thus explores several important elements of physical and psychological movement that relate to classroom management

Physical Movement

Motor Development and Maintenance

Although a cognitive decision to move may involve billions of neurons, only about a half million motor neurons are involved in activating the muscle groups that make up almost half of our body weight. Our jointed motor system with its complex brain and muscle connections provides our brain with a remarkably effective external mechanism for action. It is composed of the toe, foot, and leg system that is about half our body's length; the finger, hand, and arm system that extends our reach about 2 feet beyond our body; a flexible neck that increases the geographic range of our head's sensory receptors; and a remarkable mouth that begins digestion and also communicates through both sound and expressive facial movements.

Several brain systems (notably the parietal lobes, cerebellum, and motor cortex) coordinate the actual initiation and execution of movement, acting as a sort of virtual reality center that initially simulates projected movements to accelerate and better control our actual movements. This neuronal system constantly draws on internal models, automatic programs, and sensory feedback to analyze our current body position and movement goals as it predicts and then activates the appropriate motor commands. It is amazing how well the system predicts such things as the weight of the object, the height of the stairstep, or the distance to the target before sending out motor commands, and it is generally processing several major motor commands simultaneously! It is an excellent system, but not perfect. If it were, professional basketball players would always shoot free throws successfully, we would never spill soup on our clothing, and life would indeed be boring.

Not surprisingly, our sensitive sensory system and finely controlled movements are central to the visual, aural, and movement arts (including most sports, which are basically a dance form). The arts play an important role in our culture because (among other values) they provide a stimulating and often pleasant means for developing and maintaining our motor system up to virtuoso levels. Consider the fine motor control of a painter, the practiced pizzicato of a violinist, or the choreographed pick-and-roll of an NBA team. Because movement is so central to being human, we really ought to do it with style and grace, and the arts do enhance the development and maintenance of both choreographed and improvised movements.

Chapter 5 suggested that the development of smoothly controlled motor systems is a major priority of childhood. Suckling is almost the first mobile act of an infant, followed by the brain-outward maturation of the arm and leg systems (eating before grasping before walking). Because mobility is a central human characteristic, these innate systems must develop early at the survival level without formal instruction or even mimicry (blind children easily master walking without ever having observed it). This motor development includes specific currently ill-understood periods during which various key specialized brain systems generally develop (such as walking at about the age of 1, talking at about age 2).

Children denied the opportunity to develop a motor-driven survival skill that they would normally master with ease during its

preferred developmental period may not recover from the deprivation. A good example is the tragic case of Genie. She was 13 when
discovered hidden naked in a closet, almost totally deprived of normal language and motor development by her mentally disturbed
parents. Competent therapists who tried to undo the damage were
only marginally successful (Rymer, 1993).

Most folks realize that the cognitive and motor systems that
process language must be stimulated early and regularly to master
the local spoken and written language, and we correctly insist that
schools focus on the key elements, but communicative motor development certainly involves more than that. For example, within the
same student brain is another set of neural systems that processes
musical forms that are distinct from articulate speech. Song uses
such elements as tone, melody, harmony, and rhythm to insert important emotional overtones into a now slowed-down verbal message. Our brain's language and (verbal/nonverbal) music systems
must both be developmentally stimulated, especially those subsystems that regulate highly controlled motor activity (such as
speaking and singing, writing, and musical instrument playing).

Both communicative forms permeate our culture (and Chapter
5 suggested that music plays an especially important role during
adolescence). How can anyone justify a curriculum that seeks to
develop language but not musical capabilities? Is spelling really
biologically more important than melody when both express culturally significant sequential information?

Are our innate music networks (and other educationally ignored cognitive/motor systems) something like unwanted tonsils
or appendix tissue to be removed rather than understood and
enhanced? It is difficult to imagine how anyone involved with educational policy can have such a limited view of our brain and the
curriculum. Recall the plight of Genie previously discussed. How
many musically limited students are now emerging from school,
having had practically no competent professional development of
their innate musical ability, or for that matter, of their spatial processing centers that are so central to the visual and movement arts?
How foolish we have been in recent years to eliminate trained
teachers and programs especially tuned to such developmentally
important systems.

We are born into a very complex world with an immature brain,
one third its adult size. Because we can live in a wide variety of

environments, our sensory and motor development beyond innate survival needs tends to focus on the specific environmental demands that each brain confronts. Highly specialized and coordinated movement patterns such as those used in calligraphy, playing the violin, and tap dancing must thus be taught, and mastery is typically difficult. The importance of the early acquisition of such skills was demonstrated in a recent study of right-handed violinists (Elbert et al., 1995). Separate, specific brain areas control right- and left-hand finger movements. Violinists who began lessons before the age of 12 developed important strengths in the size and complexity of these motor areas that did not develop in nonviolinists (who had less need for the left-hand digital dexterity required in right-handed violinists) or even in good violinists who began later.

Michael Jordan, a recent basketball superstar, is another interesting example (Klawans, 1996). At the age of 31 he decided to fulfill a dream and switch to baseball. With all of his athletic ability and resolve, he did not do nearly as well as he had hoped. Throwing a basketball through a hoop requires different sensory and motor skills than hitting a 90+-mile-per-hour baseball. Even major league pitchers are not recycled into hitters when their pitching abilities wane, although they understand the game and batted during the games they pitched.

Survival-level cognitive and motor skills are universal and innate. Explicit early instruction and effort can get us beyond mere survival levels into the normal limits of human capability. Virtuoso-level abilities are highly specific and require the commitment of early extensive training. Many young people exhibit this skill-specific commitment when they continuously practice specialized skills. Call it play if you will, but Piaget suggested that play is the serious business of childhood.

Classroom activities should provide many opportunities for the development of all educationally relevant motor skills beyond mere survival. Chapter 3 reported the research that indicated that elevated levels of the neurotransmitter serotonin enhance relaxation and the calm assurance that leads to smoothly controlled and coordinated movement patterns, and such movements tend to increase one's self-esteem. Too many classrooms continue to be a pencil-driven sedentary environment that is quite removed from the complex mobility that human biology seeks and now desperately needs in an era increasingly influenced by movement technologies (such as the peculiar phenomenon of parental cars driving young people a short distance to soccer practice). It is true that students spend most of their life in nonschool settings that often encourage biological mobility, but do work with your students to create a more biologically mobile classroom.

Sound as Movement

Sound (the result of information-laden, rhythmically moving air molecules reaching eardrums) is perhaps the most common form of classroom movement. Given the size and composition of the group, classrooms tend to be relatively quiet, and teachers are expected to keep them that way. A quiet classroom and a successful language arts program are important factors when evaluating an elementary teacher's performance, despite the apparent contradiction. A considerable body of evidence (and common knowledge) indicates that the teacher typically talks as much or more as all the rest of the class put together, and teachers do not have to ask permission to talk.

Why then does classroom noise upset teachers (and it is generally high on teacher annoyance lists)? What else can one reasonably expect from a couple dozen students working together for hours in a room with many sound-reflecting hard, smooth surfaces where communication defines the very experience? Well, why not get upset by classroom noise? The sounds of normal social interaction differ considerably from the noise of distraction that draws attention away from the learning activities that brought the class together.

It is a dilemma. Most educators would be hard-pressed to precisely explain the difference between the sounds of productive classwork and distracting classroom noise, but almost all can easily differentiate between the two in an actual active classroom.

It is often possible to reduce distracting classroom noise by creating buffers that absorb sound within the room (such as strategically placed plants and fabric hangings). Experienced teachers also discover that when they speak softly, it encourages students to be quieter so they can hear better. Model and teach your students how to speak with a 12-inch, 24-inch, or 48-inch voice (the distance at which another person can easily hear comments), and then indicate during different class activities which voice is appropriate (a conversation between two students suggests 12 inches, a comment during a class discussion requires 48 inches).

Desks are typically arranged in the center of the classroom, and this compresses students and so increases distracting sounds. If you have this problem, experiment with arrangements that group desks around the edge of the room. You will spread out the sound and create a useful empty space in the middle of the room where (for example) students can assemble in chairs or on the floor in a compact circle for (quieter) discussion activities. Furthermore, you can place sound and visual buffers in the central area to reduce distracting stimuli.

Teachers tend to respond to the almost constant undercurrent of classroom sound with an ongoing string of verbal reprimands (e.g., "Quiet down now," "John and Tom, please stop your conversation and get to work," "Walk quietly to the door"). Verbal and nonverbal sounds are thus the most common classroom distraction, and continuing verbal reprimands are the most common management measure. How intriguing!

Frequently used disciplinary measures tend to be ineffective because if they were effective, teachers would not have to continually use them. So why do intelligent, experienced teachers continue to use a management technique of limited effectiveness? A sixth grader explained it beautifully:

> Well, most teachers are fair, or at least they want to be fair. They know that just asking kids to quiet down doesn't really work, but they do it anyway, because they know a few of the kids will quiet down. Then they raise their voices and holler a little bit, and some more kids quiet down. Then they threaten the noisy ones and some more quiet down. By that time they found out who the really noisy kids are, and they give them serious punishments. Now it wouldn't be fair to punish everyone for being noisy right away, because some kids are just being noisy because that's normal. So the teacher does the things that don't really work on those students to find out who they are, and then only punishes those who didn't quit when she gave them a chance. That's being fair, even if it doesn't work very well.

How eloquent. What the comment suggests is that students have a practical grasp of the inner dynamics of classroom management, and informal studies and simple observations indicate, not surprisingly, that students who frequently misbehave (and are thus central to the problem) seem to have a better grasp of management dynamics than students identified as well behaved. Because the students' perspectives of management differ from the teacher's, they can become useful collaborators on devising procedures for reducing common distractions such as classroom noise. Students consider fairness to be very important in management.

Touch, Where Movement Stops

Touch is probably the most problematic of all the movement-related issues in classroom management. We first learn the difference between ourselves and others through touch, and we continue to explore the positive and negative manifestations of tactile relationships throughout life.

Our brain and skin are the first two organs to emerge in the human embryo, and they develop out of the same layer of embryonic tissue; one side of the layer develops into our 3-pound brain, and the other into the 6-pound, 20-square-foot mantle of skin that covers our body. We can thus think of our skin as the outside layer of our brain because our sense organs are embedded in skin. Our skin is the largest organ in our body and the most sensitive to environmental dangers and opportunities because when anything physically bad happens our skin gets whacked first.

Although verbal reprimands often bounce unheard off student eardrums, physical punishment signals the absolute end of unproductive verbal interaction. Although some folks still promote spanking and other forms of physical punishment as necessary and therapeutic, it is something that occurs rarely in schools, and it tends to leave everyone dissatisfied. As the sixth grader above implied, the threat of corporal punishment typically works only with those who do not need it. Those whose behavior we wish to improve through corporal punishment tend to shrug it off as part of their continuing sometimes-you-win-sometimes-you-lose battle with the system.

The discussion earlier in this chapter argued that neural systems that process language, music, and motor systems must be stimulated in order to reach their potential. Similarly, the gentle holding, hugging, caressing, and nuzzling that most children receive within their extended family during their preschool years helps activate and mature neural systems that enhance physically close relationships. It is common knowledge now that children who do not receive such loving tactile stimulation suffer from the deprivation. The adolescent years are another such important period, one in which (generally nonfamily) touch and other forms of physical closeness enhance sexual maturation.

We have a school problem with touching during the entire K-12 span. Many (touch-deprived) students who would benefit much from positive teacher hugs probably will not receive them in the current climate because educators are concerned about potential charges of child molestation and sexual harassment and simply do not want to take the risk. It is a sad problem without a simple solution.

Student physical aggression is another problem without a simple solution. So many school and nonschool events can trigger the stress that triggered the shoving or the fight that it is difficult to predict when physical aggression will occur and who will be involved. Because relatively innocuous brushing-to-bumping contacts can quickly escalate into push-back and fighting behaviors if a currently short-tempered student was brushed, it is always wise to organize school movement patterns so that they minimize unwanted physical contact. When a fight begins, the best strategy is to quickly physically separate the fighters until tempers cool and you have an opportunity to determine what caused the problem. Because this is something that will occur periodically during the year, discuss the problem with your students and teach them how to immediately try to talk the fighters into separating if no teacher is readily available to take over. The advantage of creating such a rational strategy is that it raises a typically unconscious action to the level of conscious thought, and this in itself may reduce the number of class fights.

Similarly, student sexual harassment through fondling and other unwanted tactile contacts is another problem that has intensified in recent years. Many folks used to laugh it off as inept attempts at romancing, but no more.

Most schools have now developed programs or implemented published programs that purport to train students in assertiveness, to reduce the stereotyping and harassment of targeted individuals and small groups of students, to teach anger management, and the

like. How sad that it has become necessary to legalize and insti-
tutionalize such a fundamental human relationship as touch, but
that is the way it is. Furthermore, we do not want good-touch-bad-
touch rhetoric to frighten young children away from positive contacts with adults, and we do not want the informal rough-and-
tumble of school life that is generally positive to escalate into the
bullying and fighting that is almost always negative, but that is the
way it is. It is thus very important that we truly involve students in
the discussion of such problems and in the proposal and implementation of solutions. They are part of the problem, so they ought to be
part of the solution.

Change as Psychological Movement

Our large frontal lobes allow us to experience movement as a psychological as well as a physical phenomenon. People physically
move from one community to another, but they also then change
jobs, and they may psychologically shift to a different career level.
Children are also involved in such career-related family moves,
and they are often unhappy about it. Moves can be especially difficult for children whose parents' vocation requires multiple moves
(such as those in the military, large corporations, the clergy, and
sports). Furthermore, current vocational patterns suggest that most
people will change jobs (and even vocations) several times during
their career, so the problem will probably continue. If it is a positive
career-related move to another community, the parental delight
over the move may further exacerbate their children's unhappiness
(as occurred once within our family during a career-related move
that delighted my wife and me but not our children).

Our brain responds most strongly to high-contrast information, and it can activate stress responses when such information
seems threatening. Holmes and Rahe (1967) found that the most
stressful (high-contrast) life changes involve the loss of family and
friends and the prospect of having to make new friends, so children
who move from their community and school experience a lot of
psychologically threatening goodby-and-hello activity. Students
who depart and arrive during the school year are therefore generally experiencing a period of high stress (and perhaps the variety of

physical ailments that often accompany high stress). The situation is similar with students who will move or have moved during the summer. Chapter 5 introduced the concept of a responsive curriculum, and the discussion that follows suggests that the physical and psychological shifts that students experience are certainly an important part of this curriculum and ought to be recognized in the classroom if it is appropriate.

It is important to help young people make the transition as smoothly as possible. In our family's case, a generous phone policy and trips back to see friends helped the transition, but e-mail and the Internet now provide marvelous, inexpensive keep-in-touch possibilities that did not exist a few years ago (and school-to-school e-mail connections during a transition work well for students without a computer at home).

It is very difficult to provide extended support to transient students in schools with an unusually high turnover rate during the school year, but a class that goes through the process only a few times a year can be quite helpful to their departing classmates.

Encourage students who are moving to check out their new community on the Internet and in the public library and to request material on the community from the Chamber of Commerce. Check to see if any staff or students in your school have lived in the community to which your student is moving and bring the two together. If your student's family has already secured housing, and know which school your student will attend, contact his or her future class via e-mail and begin the student's "hello" process prior to arrival. Encourage your student to prepare a class report on the community because such a project typically develops a more positive attitude about the move.

Continue class contact via e-mail after the move. The contacts will taper off as your former student develops new friends, but close friends will probably stay in contact longer via e-mail if you encourage it. Send a copy of the room diary (see Suggested Activities, Chapter 5) to students who moved during the school year or (if you do not develop a room diary) develop a collaborative end-of-the-year report to send to all students who moved during the year.

It is equally important to create procedures for welcoming new students into your classroom. The entire class is new at the beginning of the school year, but some students already know each other because they were classmates last year, and/or are neighborhood friends. Others will have moved into the community during the summer or are transferring from another community school.

> Schedule many group activities during the first weeks, mixing the already acquainted with the truly new in a variety of groupings. Ask the new students to tell the class about their previous community and friends. Develop activities that help students identify their interests and abilities and then create class groups that reflect such commonalities.
>
> Divide your class into host committees of four students. Each committee should serve for 2 weeks to welcome and assist any students who arrive during their tenure. Each committee would thus serve about three times during the year. These formal first friends may not become the permanent friends of the new students, but developing some kind of system to help students get acquainted certainly smoothes the process.

Death, divorce, and a major drop in family income are examples of other psychological moves that can greatly grieve students. They often signal the end of the life a person had been living. Students may or may not want to tell you about their problems, but teachers commonly become aware of the significant life changes their students are experiencing.

Part of the problem that children confront is that their primary caregivers are often also traumatized by the event and so may not be able to effectively help them through the grief process. Children, feeling a mixed bag of experiences and emotions (such as loss, betrayal, anger, sadness), may not know how to respond and so withdraw. Adults may interpret this as a lack of feeling or that the child is doing fine, but the reality is that the child is typically devastated and confused. It is also important to realize that a loss that may seem trivial to an adult (such as the death of a pet or the loss of a favorite toy) may be very important to your student.

Let your grieving student know by words and action that you are aware of and genuinely concerned about the situation. Carefully observe your student's behavior and always make time to listen when your student wants to talk. Be sensitive to different students and situations, a family death typically does not embarrass a child, but a divorce or the parental loss of a job might. Bibliotherapy can often help grieving students because such children's books allow readers to privately explore their personal grief through the story's narrative (Rousell, 1992). Ask librarians for suggestions of good storybooks that focus on the loss your student is experiencing. Finally, the effort expended to create a caring classroom really pays off when students grieve. They discover that people they live with 6 hours a day are developing into a support group for each other, and the grieving student can see others providing the support that he or she would provide to classmates if the conditions were reversed.

This chapter began with the joyful centrality of movement in our lives, and it concludes with the sad ending of movement that occurs in such events as hitting and dying. Movement is an intriguing enigma. Sometimes, so many people want to simultaneously move quickly along a street that gridlock seriously slows the process, and anger seethes. Conversely, people may later line the sidewalks of the same street in a celebratory mood to observe a parade that also moves very slowly. We will spend several minutes driving through a mall parking lot to find a space near an entrance when we could have immediately parked slightly further away and walked to the entrance and back in much less time. People are impressed by television commercials of sports utility vehicles bouncing over rugged terrain, buy one, and never drive it off paved roads. People save money for a vacation in order to get away from it all, travel 1,000 miles to another city, stay in a franchise motel, eat in franchise restaurants, visit franchise-dominated malls, and see films—all of which are available in their home community. Why did they leave home? When we are here, we often want to be there. When we are young we want to look grown up, and when we are old we want things to look young. We truly are crazy about movement!

Suggested Activities

The activities below explore some of the slow-to-fast movement patterns that occur across a school year and so can spark discussions about the concept of movement that could lead to management adaptations. Because movement combines space and time, some of these activities are also appropriate for exploring space and time.

Weight and Height

Growth is so gradual that most of us are unaware of it. If you measure and/or weigh the entire class once a week and graph the total, the graph will provide the class with an amazing and amusing view of their total growth over the year. (A fifth-grade class of 25 students may grow a combined total of 6-plus feet and add 200 pounds during the course of the school year, almost the equivalent of a couple of additional students.) Primary grades can graph their total weekly loss of teeth, and other classes may come up with other interesting things in their lives that can be graphed in their weekly totality. These graphs are not a good activity with a class that contains students who might be sensitive about the factors being measured and graphed.

An Event Clock

Post a strip of paper about 1 foot wide and 7 feet long on a wall. Divide the length from top down into 15-minute intervals from the beginning to the end of the school day (write 8:00, 8:15, 8:30, etc. down the left side). Ask your students to notice events that occur about the same time every day (a passing mail truck, a scheduled commercial plane flying overhead, the first whiff of the cafeteria smells, a class going to the gym). Check each candidate event for several days to ensure its regularity and then insert the event into the closest 15-minute slot on the event clock. The clock will usually fill up with predictable events by the end of the school year, but it may become a real challenge in May to locate predictable events for the few unfilled slots. The activity gives you two classroom clocks: a chronological clock and an amusing event clock that charts how things move across the day ("The mailman has arrived, so it is just about time for PE").

Lumber Use

Give each of your students a pencil the first day of school. The writing part of a pencil (up to the metal eraser cap) is 6.75 inches, so it is relatively easy to measure how much pencil space the class will use during a week.

Place a pad by the wastebasket, and ask students to make a tally for every sheet of paper they throw in the wastebasket. Graph the amount of paper that moves into and out of your classroom.

Move It

It is fun to develop timed competitions in which teams of students try to move something through an obstacle course without actually touching it. For example, give each of three team members a drinking straw and the challenge to use the straws to move a ping pong ball over a prescribed course. They can blow on the ball, collaborate on trying to pick it up and carry it with their three straws, or devise any other approach that does not involve team members actually touching it. Your class will devise all sorts of other imaginative challenges that limit the resources they can use to move something, such as using a yard of string to move a soccer ball up a flight of stairs.

Help your students discover that these activities do naturally what video games do electronically, move something (such as the Mario Brothers or Yoshi) from here to there in the face of obstacles. But then, don't golf, tennis, baseball, and hockey also use implements to move objects from here to there?

Moving Mail to Locate Someone

Select a friend who lives far removed from your community. Provide your class with some information about your friend (city, vocation, interests, memberships, etc. [but no phone/address]). The students' task is to identify someone who may know your friend. They can also ask their parents for help, and the chances are good that you will get several viable candidates: "My uncle lives in Boston, so maybe he knows her," "My Dad works for the same company here that she works for in Chicago, so maybe he knows her," "We belong to the same church, so maybe someone in our family knows someone who belongs to that church in Seattle." Select the best of the proposed candidates and send something similar to the letter below. Surprisingly, it normally takes fewer than 10 letters to reach anyone in the country through this activity (similar to 20

Example 6.1. Sample Moving Mail Activity Letter

Our class is trying to discover how many mail contacts it takes to locate and get a letter from us to a total stranger. This is what we know about_____

Provide information:

We think that you might know him or her, or someone who might know him or her. Would you please send this letter to someone you know who you think might actually know the person we are trying to contact (or might know someone who might know the person).

Write below why you sent the letter to that person. We have enclosed enough stamps to keep this letter going until it reaches _____. When we have reached _____, and he or she returns everything to us, we will send you a copy of the journey this letter followed. Thanks so much.

1. First letter:
Name _____
Address _____
Your reason for sending it to the next person:

2. Second letter:
Name _____
Address _____
Your reason for sending it to the next person:

Etc.

Questions, which usually only takes a few questions to identify any of thousands of possibilities).

E-mail transmission has now reached such a broad distribution that it is probably possible to carry out this activity via e-mail. Use this activity as an introduction to the study of such things as how library catalog systems are organized to locate books, how to locate information when you do not know much about it, and how information moves through the Internet.

Chapter ❼

Exploring Range as a Dimension of Classroom Management

We could theoretically live decades beyond our current human life span and confront any possible challenge, but that capability would come at an enormous biological cost: back-up and regenerative systems for everything, a fail-safe immune system and protective mechanisms for larger external and internal dangers, and a much larger bodybrain than we currently have to continuously support all this extra capability.

We could similarly design our machines to last far longer and function more efficiently than they typically do, but it is doubtful that we could then afford them. For example, consider the current cost of the very best engineered automobiles and the high per-mile cost of maintaining them. The more complex the task of a technology, the greater the maintenance costs and potential for an eventual costly breakdown. On the other hand, we can use important but simple limited-use technologies such as spoons and bottle openers for many decades without any need for repair.

We humans have many complex body parts and systems, but we can still live to about 100 years, eat a wide variety of plants and animals, live in crowded communities, and survive in a thermal range of more than 100 degrees. Our maintenance costs for being able to live a long life in a worldwide ecological range are very high, though, compared with early humans who lived less than half our average life span in a far simpler environment. Consider how much of our energy (translated into income) we use to pay for such needs as food, clothing, shelter, travel, and medical costs. We have further used our considerable cognitive ability to develop technologies that compensate for our biological limitations. For example, we have developed travel, shelter, medical, and food preparation technologies to augment our bodybrain's capabilities and to extend our ecological range and life span.

The trade-off in both biology and technology is to balance cost and benefit, to provide for whatever is necessary to carry out the desired function, but to not go very far beyond that. Recent lawsuits against car manufacturers have alleged that the companies deliberately used cheaper parts than what was available, and the malfunction of the cheap parts caused the accidents that killed the driver and/or passengers. The decision was allegedly made because the manufacturer determined that it would cost less to settle the lawsuits from a potentially small number of accidents than to purchase the more expensive part for the many cars it intended to manufacture. We are appalled at such reasoning, but then we do try to spend as little money as possible when purchasing a car.

Schools must constantly make similarly difficult cost and benefit decisions. Our patrons expect us to accomplish a lot (a wide benefit range), but to do it as cheaply and efficiently as possible (a narrow cost range). It is unfair but common for them to then complain when we are forced to make choices that eliminate staff and programs that would benefit their children. If we want the cost/benefit ratio to favor economy, we must realize that a cheap car is a cheap car, and a cheap education is a cheap education. It should not be difficult to understand that a reduced investment in something also typically reduces its range of possibilities and overall effectiveness.

Could schools accomplish everything one could hope for if we had unlimited resources and staff? Probably not. Expending money to expand the effective range of something does not necessarily ensure perfection. Like cars, we humans have some critically important systems (such as circulation and respiration) that seem to give out eventually, whereas other systems (such as the skin and skeleton) typically continue to function well at our death. The body and engine of cars and humans are excellent, but they are not perfect. We can spend a lot of money to maintain the health of our heart and/or lungs, and practically no money on our skin and bones, and still die of heart or lung failure. Schools can similarly expend a lot of energy on students who are well below the normal range in ability and/or behavior, but that does not ensure success in moving them into the normal range, if that is the goal. It also does not mean that we should simply give up on them.

The biological cost/benefit ratio suggests that the general biological imperative for plants and animals is to stay alive long enough and do whatever it takes to get into the gene pool. We bear dependent children, so we have a bodybrain that is generally up to the task of staying alive through our reproductive cycle and then long enough beyond it to complete the extended rearing of any children we have (and as a social species, we also participate in rearing the children of others). A great serendipity of the recent biologically expensive advances in medicine, diet, shelter, and so forth is that many of us now live long enough to also enjoy our grandchildren and great-grandchildren (which my grandparents could not do), but it does take us beyond our normal biological expectations.

What is biologically possible and what is culturally appropriate are the two principal issues we humans face as we compete to stay alive and get into the gene pool (culturally appropriate behavior tending to enhance mating attractiveness). The concepts of biological possibility and cultural appropriateness presuppose that our capabilities and behavior operate within somewhat definable functional and acceptable personal and social ranges.

This chapter thus focuses on the final behavioral element in the biological and cultural underpinnings of classroom management. Biological systems function through the expenditure of energy within our space/time world, which generally causes physical and psychological movement within biological and cultural ranges.

This examination finally gets us into what are probably the three most important of Gardner's (1998) nine categories of intelligence: intrapersonal, interpersonal, and existential intelligence—Who am I? Who are these people around me? What does it mean to exist?

Because issues surrounding classroom management focus principally on determining the reasonable range of possible and appropriate movement (or behavior) in a classroom, it is important for educators and students to understand (and to explore) the concept of biological and cultural range as they relate to identity. The two examples that follow should spark exploratory thought and discussion.

1. An individual light fixture typically functions within a very narrow light production range. It is either on or off. It has no almost-on state, and most have no dimming capabilities. We decide how much light we want the fixture to produce and then use a bulb with that intensity. Similarly, an individual neuron activates only if the incoming molecular information reaches the cell's current firing threshold, and it remains inactive otherwise. It is a narrow-range, all-or-nothing operating system that, like a light bulb, is tuned to the needs of its specific task.

Conversely, our brain's complex of more than 100 billion neurons allows it to function more like a room full of on/off light fixtures of various intensities that together can create a wide range of light intensities and shadows. I sat transfixed in a theater yesterday as the complex lighting system (with its on/off, dimming, placement, and color capabilities) intensified and enhanced the positive-to-negative range of the elements in a play that would have been a considerably different experience had the stage lighting been severely limited and unchanging. The story would have been told, but much of the theatrical magic would have been absent. On the other hand, spectacular lighting that overwhelms the play can be counterproductive. Just right (whatever that is) is best. Tune the system to the task.

Our brain's total level of activation similarly depends on which and how many neurons are actively responding to the current challenges. An individual neuron is thus a very limited on/off system, but a total brain has a very wide range of behavioral states. Similarly, an entire classroom full of individually limited brains sparks thoughts of the wide range of constantly changing light intensities that highlight the stage area where a play is being performed. The constantly shifting behavioral intensities that so characterize classroom management problems may thus be the theatrical magic of a school day, highlighting individual activity within the range of constantly changing positive-to-negative curricular and behavioral elements. What are the possible and appropriate ranges of intensity? That is the problem a theatrical director and classroom teacher constantly confront, and fortunately, there is no one way to light a play or to manage a classroom. How dull life would be if things were that simple and absolute.

2. Range problems are everywhere. Let us use something as mundane as this page to explore another element of the concept of range. The words on this page could have been printed so they would reach to all four edges, but it is not possible to print them beyond the edges. The page dimensions thus define the possible range. Although it is possible to print to the edge, we typically leave a margin between text and edge because it aids in binding the pages if it is a multiple page document, and margins allow for margin notes. Whatever the original reason for margins, they are familiar and so we have become comfortable with them and expect them.

The issue of the size of the margin gets to the heart of appropriateness. One-inch margins are probably the default width (and a requirement for certain manuscripts), but we often reduce the margins to fit all the text of a letter that is slightly longer than a page onto a single page, or we expand the margins to center a short letter on a page. We may also extend the margin size of a small section of text to set it off from the rest. So margin decisions may be based on an artificial requirement, or on what is aesthetically pleasing to whomever gets to determine the margin size.

We further commonly change the margins for headings and to signal the beginning and ending of a paragraph. The first (indented) line of the paragraph has a wider left margin, and the end of the paragraph often stops short of the normal right margin. That is the common practice, but it is also appropriate to double space (without indenting) to separate paragraphs.

Suppose someone decides to simply print an extended manuscript as a single long paragraph, sentence following sentence following sentence, and simply uses an icon (such as *) to identify the first sentence of each new paragraph. The text would not have changed at all, and the signal for a new paragraph is certainly clear. It is readable, but most of us would not like it. It is a possible but unfamiliar procedure, and so we would probably consider it inappropriate. But why? Just because.

It may be that the cost/benefit ratio concept is so deeply ingrained in us that we automatically and often unconsciously compute it in most challenges we face, even such as how easy it is to read the text on a page compared to the value of the material. Our cost/benefit computations typically lead us to a comfortable acceptable range, even though we realize that our acceptable range is quite subjective, and perhaps narrower or wider than the acceptable range of others.

In a complex society, some want to extend a given normal behavioral range, others do not. Think of a freeway with posted speed limits of 45 to 65 miles per hour. Most people do not consider it serious if someone travels beyond the range at 44 or 66, but traveling at 30 or 80 may attract honking and gesturing (as ironically will driving in the passing lane at exactly the posted speed). Folks who travel the freeway at 75 rather than 65 save only about 10 minutes on a 100-mile trip. It is perhaps hardly worth the risk and effort, but it is understandable if the cost/benefit goal is not to save 10 minutes but rather to extend one's velocity range. My favorite rear bumper sticker in this category is "I may be slow, but I'm ahead of you."

Normal. Familiar. Comfortable. We consider these very important interrelated factors when we make decisions. They all assume a somewhat flexible range of what is acceptable, and so they allow us to quickly (and often unconsciously) choose among alternatives. Things do not have to be exact, just close and within our comfort range. If one color is not available, we will take another (if color is not the critical factor).

Advertising often exploits our preference for familiar comfortable normality. In the advertising world, images we can easily relate to confront familiar problems. Everything is normal in the scenario except the product, which is abnormally cheaper (cost) and/or better (benefit) than its competition—a little abnormal seasoning in a big pot of comfortable familiar normality. Better yet, let us connect a comfortable children's film to our burgers and fries, or a familiar television football analyst to our hardware chain, or a normal activity like driving a car to our roaring-up-the-mountain sports utility vehicle and our ad will spice up comfort, familiarity, and normality with a little celebrity and excitement. Still better, tie a product icon to the entire scenario, and then all we have to do is display the swoosh or the golden arches, and everyone will settle comfortably into familiar normality.

Figure 7.1 illustrates the concept of range. It identifies a normal range area and high/low abnormal levels separated by leaky horizontal lines (semipermeable membranes, no less) that illustrate the

Figure 7.1. Biological and Cultural Normality and Abnormality

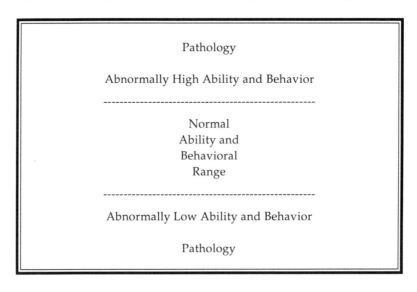

frequent difficulty of clearly establishing the point at which normality becomes abnormality. Abnormal performance can become a pathology if it moves far enough beyond the normal range, and anything at that level is typically more expensive to make (a critical machine part that could kill someone if it malfunctions) or to maintain (penitentiary inmates). Technological assistance (such as medication or a wheelchair) is often used to improve the behavior of a low-performing abnormality, and to dampen above-normal performance that is negative (such as ADHD medication). Above-normal behavior that is considered positive (virtuoso behavior) is also often technologically augmented (such as with food supplements and exercise equipment for athletes) in an attempt to move the behavior even further beyond normality.

Biologically Possible Ranges

As suggested earlier, it is not biologically sound for any human ability or behavior to function within an almost limitless range. The cost/benefit ratio just does not compute. The Olympic Games represent one glorious attempt to extend the range of human movement. Some folks spend much of their youth trying to lengthen the human jumping range by one more inch, but most of us who want to go higher than we currently are simply use a ladder. It is an issue of personal identity.

We can assemble a normally distributed collection of students along almost any ability and performance range. For whatever reason, more than half will typically fall within the defined normal range, and the others will spread out into the high and low abnormal ranges—the bell-shaped curve. It is possible that the normal range of many abilities eventually emerged (in some ill-understood way) out of a biologically favorable cost/benefit ratio related to the general imperative to stay alive and get into the gene pool, and that is why so many folks end up within the normal range. Being in the normal range in that ability would simplify our life and reduce the energy we need to carry out a task that we are now biologically tuned into. By extension, having a whole classroom full of normally behaving students certainly reduces the energy a teacher must expend in working with them.

We have tended to put more of our energy into designing educational programs for normal students than for those abnormally high and low. Again, the cost/benefit ratio often favors such a focus for teachers. The much larger number of students in the normal range in an ability have provided our profession with many years of useful normative information on student capability and instructional preference. Much of this is folklore knowledge, but it drives much of what we do. If most of our students are more or less capable of carrying out our planned (normal range) instructional task, it is almost like we only have to teach one multihead student, and so a one-size-fits-all instructional approach provides us a great cost/benefit ratio. What if we misjudge the group's ability? Not to worry. Students have this marvelous feedback system called misbehavior to let us know if we have overshot or undershot their ability and interest range. Tweak the lesson plan and continue.

Unfortunately, designing curriculum and instruction principally for students in the normal range almost ensures by definition that much of it will be too difficult for the abnormally low and not challenging enough for the abnormally high. Grades and disciplinary measures are, alas, one way of transferring the blame for low performance to the student. A major task in the years ahead will be to develop better diagnostic tools of student ability, and to develop individualized computer programs in curricular areas in which we currently teach an individually mastered skill (such as spelling or the multiplication tables) in a whole class setting, when there is nothing social about the multiplication tables. Whole-class instruction could then focus on true socially oriented curricular areas and issues, such as the arts and humanities, in which a performance standard is of less concern than the exploration of different ways to confront a concept. Science and social studies projects are another area in which a broad range of student ability can function effectively in a group setting, and we have yet to develop a truly effective social behavior curriculum. Finally, this book has argued throughout that teachers can reduce many of their problems by simply involving their students in the design and execution of as many curricular, instructional, and management tasks as possible. Doing this does not eliminate problems; it just trades one set of problems for another, but they are more stimulating problems.

U.S. schools have invested far more money per student in trying to increase the performance of the abnormally low than the abnormally high. It may be a matter of (perhaps unconsciously) wanting to move the abnormally low into normal levels and of being somewhat disinterested in moving the abnormally high even further from normality.

Singapore, on the other hand, invests heavily in programs for talented and gifted students in the belief that it is investing in the economic and political future of its country by providing its best students with the best educational opportunities. The U.S. decision may partially reflect the belief that the mark of a society is in how it treats those who are most in need of help. Note that two economically successful countries computed the educational cost/benefit ratio differently. The ideal policy would obviously be to create excellent programs across the entire normal and abnormal range (but it is difficult to negotiate cost/benefit ratios in a highly politicized institution).

Why are some in the abnormal range? For a long time, people thought motivation and perseverance were the key elements, and the abnormally high and low were the cause of their own condition. Recent developments suggest that it is more complex than that. Let us examine just one factor in ability and behavior: neurochemical normality and abnormality.

Some 60 neurotransmitter systems play key roles in regulating cognitive activity, and abnormally high or low basal levels of a neurotransmitter can affect ability and performance in the areas the neurotransmitter helps to regulate. Dopamine is an important neurotransmitter that regulates various behaviors. Low dopamine levels have been associated with Parkinson's disease and attention deficit disorders. Conversely, high dopamine levels have been associated with such maladies as schizophrenia, Tourette's syndrome, and Obsessive Compulsive Disorder. Medical interventions seek to move abnormal levels into the normal range, for example, L-Dopa and other medications are prescribed to boost dopamine levels for Parkinson patients, and neuroleptics to reduce dopamine levels in schizophrenics.

Chapters 3 and 6 discussed serotonin, which plays an important role in regulating movement. Low serotonin levels lead to uncoordinated, awkward movements that tend to lower self-esteem (given the social importance of our motor system), and high serotonin levels lead to smoothly coordinated movements that tend to enhance one's self-esteem. Furthermore, low serotonin levels have been associated with such maladies as depression and bulimia, and high serotonin levels with anorexia. The fluexitine antidepressants (such as Prozak) boost serotonin effectiveness, but as indicated earlier, we have also long self-medicated with alcohol, carbohydrates, and herbal remedies (such as St. Johns Wort) to boost moderately low serotonin levels.

Given that the other five dozen neurotransmitters also play important roles in determining a wide variety of abilities and behaviors, it is becoming more obvious that if basal neurotransmitter levels are at least partially innate, not everyone has a biologically equal opportunity to function easily within the normal optimum neurochemical range, and this should certainly affect classroom management expectations and practices. The biological energy the chemically abnormal students must expend to function within a school's preferred normal behavioral range will reduce the energy they have available for other functions such as what is needed for curricular tasks.

When chemical systems are imbalanced, the point of a medical intervention is to get the systems back in chemical balance and not to blame or punish the patient. Similarly, when classroom behavior is inappropriate, the principle point of the management intervention should be to restore behavioral balance in student and class. Management procedures that do this focus on helping the student(s) to understand the logical consequences of the behavior and to repair what went wrong rather than on punishment. It comes down to this: If something is broken, fix it rather than complain about it.

Abnormality in an area is not necessarily totally negative. Chapter 4 suggested that an abnormally low ability in one arena may lead to a compensating strength in a related area, a biologically sensible solution for an organism that needs to combine all its resources as best it can to function effectively. For example, some people whose brains cannot rapidly process high-contrast visual information (such as reading black words on a white page) have abnormal spatial abilities that manifest themselves in superior performance in athletics and the visual arts. We are fascinated by such virtuoso abnormalities and often pay them well to entertain us, despite their inadequacies in other performance areas.

The increased interest in such developments as cooperative learning, multiple intelligences, and learning styles attests to our profession's growing awareness that biological diversity itself can be a valuable property in a social group. If the different overlapping ability ranges in a class are respected for what they can provide, the aggregate of the individual ranges will expand the corporate range at no increased biological cost.

The ability level of most bodybrain systems is generally in the abnormally low range at birth. Some systems, such as circulation and respiration, must be functionally normal at birth, and some survival abilities, such as to suckle, come on line almost immediately after birth with no prior experience or instruction.

We can move our hands and legs at birth, but we cannot grasp or walk. Mobility is an important human capability, so, as Chapter 6 suggested, our motor system develops quickly from the low-abnormal level into the normal range. Most children walk by the age of 1 year. The maturation of most aspects of the motor system across the normal ability range is an important first-decade task.

One of our more intriguing cognitive abilities is to abstract one property out of an object regardless of what the object is. For example, even a small child can recognize the redness of a rose or a wagon, the roundness of a ball or a plate. Similarly, we can easily determine the quantity of a collection of objects (such as three boxes) regardless of differences in size, shape, use, and so forth. Recent discoveries suggest that this ability to enumerate is processed in a left (and probably also right) hemisphere brain area called the inferior parietal cortex (or angular gyrus) at the juncture of the occipital, temporal, and parietal lobes (Butterworth, 1999). We can determine the quantity of up to four objects with a quick glance (called subitizing), but we must count out larger quantities (and we generally count by ones, twos, or threes). Check it out with various collections of objects in the room to see which ones you can quantify with a quick noncounting glance.

Four-month-old infants readily differentiate among such small quantities. This seemingly innate ability represents the lower edge of our normal ability range in processing quantity. The neuronal networks that process quantities up to four thus become our mathematical womb. Neuronal systems near our brain's numerical module are recruited through childhood and beyond to expand the range of our ability to quantify from simple counting (aided by our fingers, which are also represented in the parietal lobes) to arithmetic computation to more complex mathematical problems.

Neurons in this cortical area were more densely packed than normal in Albert Einstein's brain. Butterworth (1999) reports several cases of people who suffered highly specific losses in numerical ability because of a stroke in this region that only destroyed certain specialized neurons. One woman lost her ability to subitize and could not count beyond four. Mathematics is a very complex human capability, but it all emerges from a simple innate brain module and its cognitive properties.

It is thus not surprising that we are generally most comfortable and effective when manipulating the lower numbers that were with us at birth. Primary teachers have long realized that it is easier for children to learn such multiplication facts as 2×3 than 9×7, despite the fact that the two memory tasks are similar. We further tend to reduce large complex quantities to small simpler sets, and especially to sets of three (Father, Son, Holy Ghost; id, ego, superego; legislative, executive, judicial). When asked why people tend to group complex phenomena into three categories, intelligence theorist Robert Sternberg (of Triarchic Brain Theory fame) wryly responded, "Well, there are three reasons. . . ."

To revisit and expand on our developmental trajectory briefly introduced in Chapter 4, we have a modular brain and all cognitive abilities begin with a basic, survival-level version of the mature module that processes the abilities. The environment stimulates this protosystem, and it tends to develop quickly initially with limited instruction and effort from an abnormally low level into the low-normal range. For example, we are absolutely fascinated by the rapid development of speech during the preschool years, from random babbling to articulate speech (with no explicit instruction in such language complexities as prepositional phrases and plurals). Mastery is enhanced by a rich verbal environment in which the names of things are often visually associated with the objects and actions. A parent says "Drink your milk out of this cup" while giving the child the cup.

Certain brain systems of some children are initially much less competent than normal. A child's auditory system can normally recognize sounds that are only 10 milliseconds (ms) apart. Because stop consonants (such as b, p, and k) require 40 ms and vowels 100 ms, a normal auditory system can easily separate and process the various phonemes in a word, and so such children's phonemic systems mature quickly in the welter or words they constantly hear. Conversely, language learning delayed (LLD) children have an auditory system that can only recognize sounds that are maybe 250 ms apart (a quarter of a second), so words are just jumbled sounds to them. Speech development becomes seriously delayed. Chapter 1 mentioned the Fast For Word (1997) program as a successful intervention that uses videogame technology to speed up auditory processing in such children, to move them into the normal range needed to process speech. It is probable that many other computerized skill development technologies will emerge in the foreseeable future, tuned to the very specific developmental needs of the entire range of normal and abnormal students.

More complex aspects of a cognitive ability do not come as easily and generally require explicit instruction and extended practice to make the neural connections that mature the system. Although speech seems to emerge naturally, reading must be explicitly taught because it requires visual and auditory connections that are far more abstract. Translating "Drink your milk out of this cup" into a collection of vertical, horizontal, diagonal, and curved lines on a sheet of paper with no cup in sight does not enhance immediate mastery.

The situation is similar with other abilities. Walking is almost automatic, but tap dancing must be taught and is mastered with difficulty. The startle reflex is innate, but children have to be taught how to cross busy streets and avoid sharp things. Very young children use a melody to easily memorize our alphabetic sequence of 26 unrelated letters, but they have to be taught how to play a violin.

Cognitive ranges have an upper-normal limit, and we tend to use augmenting technologies when faced with mastering a task that requires effort beyond a comfortable biological cost/benefit ratio. So children who mentally mastered the multiplication tables up to 12 use a paper-and-pencil equation or a calculator to multiply larger numbers. Children who can run quite fast for short distances use skates and bicycles to travel faster and farther. Children who easily learned the difficult alphabet sequence easily prefer to use a phone book instead of memorizing all their friends' phone numbers.

As suggested earlier, virtuosos and savants expend considerable energy to extend performance in an area well beyond the normal human range. A virtuoso is superior in one ability and at least within the normal range in most others. A savant is superior in one ability and is generally below normal in most other abilities. Many savants are autistic. Such superior performance often comes at the expense of other abilities, as the cost/benefit ratio suggests. Because much of our cognitive energy is directed toward processing social skills, the networks that process social skills (interpersonal intelligence) would be the most likely to suffer in the neuronal competitions, when some other specific ability is developed far beyond the normal range. Autism exhibits a serious social deficit, and virtuosos often (but certainly not always) exhibit social deficiencies lauded by the masses, but perhaps not by their family and associates.

Culturally Appropriate Ranges

Being biologically able to do something differs from the issue of whether we should do it. The discussion immediately above raises serious questions about the intense training required of children who seek (or whose parents seek) world-class status in some endeavor in which they have considerable ability. I am amazed by what children can do in the Olympics, for example, but I am also concerned about the loss in social development that results from intense individualized training and about the long-range effects of such training on an immature body pushed well beyond its normal range.

Ability is an individual biological phenomenon, but appropriateness typically involves behavior with strong social and cultural overtones. Like ability, the appropriateness of various behaviors extend along the normal and abnormal range illustrated in Figure 7.1.

Children typically grow up in an intensely social environment in which they constantly receive (often conflicting) messages about appropriate behavior from parents and peers. A social species depends on a somewhat equitable sharing of effort and resources, and so our culture strongly promotes a tit-for-tat mentality in children as a central element of social development. Any parent will attest that it is not an easy sell—the child grumbles at the request to do a minor chore only hours after the parent made some major desired purchase for the child. One problem with getting young children to freely share is that their life involves a very unequal dependent relationship. Others give and they take, and they get used to that arrangement. It is thus not surprising that children are self-centered.

A cooperative approach to classroom management moves students into an arena beyond the informality of their family and involves them in complex social problems that will enhance their understanding of cost/benefit ratios and help them develop a tit-for-tat orientation. It is important for our culture that children mature into altruistic adults who are able and willing to contribute their share and beyond for the common good. The school is simply an excellent laboratory for developing this.

We certainly all know adults who have not matured beyond their childhood self-centeredness. They often insist, for example, that governmental services be increased and taxes decreased despite the irrationality of their position. When challenged, they tend to ridicule governmental inefficiency to bolster a weak argument that it is easy to accomplish more with less. (How many bureaucrats does it take to screw in a lightbulb? Two: one to reassure the citizens that the problem is being solved and another to screw the bulb into a water faucet.) It is important for us to realize that all such critics went through our school system and that the next potential set is currently sitting at classroom desks. How much better it is to help them to understand the complexity of social processes now than to be very frustrated later by their simplistic complaints and solutions.

We use verbal and nonverbal means to communicate our assessment of the appropriateness of other people's behavior. As the person's behavior moves toward the negative end of our range, we use frowns and reprimands, and when the behavior moves across the line into the abnormally inappropriate range, we shift to stronger expressions of anger and disgust. Conversely, as a person's behavior becomes better than normal, we use smiles and encouragement, and when it becomes abnormally positive, we break out in laughter and effuse praise. Finally, if our behavior is more-or-less appropriate for years on end, we generally get a framed certificate upon retirement (in my case, with my name misspelled).

It is in the self-interest of children to become proficient at reading the language and body language of their significant adults in order to determine the current range of appropriate behavior and their position in it. Children who live in a family with a clearly defined constant normal range learn to tune their behavior to expectations they understand. Children who live with inconsistent parents often have no clear consistent guide to what is appropriate. Both kinds of children will constantly explore the edges of appropriateness (just as adults go slightly over the speed limit and show up a bit late for work and do other things to discover how far they can go over the line without reprimand). The children in the secure environment learn from their forays to the edge of the normal range, but the other children do not because the range constantly shifts in their home.

Getting caught going over the line is not necessarily negative in a child's life if it helps clarify the point at which appropriate behavior becomes inappropriate. Calmly discussing the logical consequences of the behavior is the best way to help children understand why their behavior is inappropriate and repair the damage they caused.

Children bring to school what they have learned at home, and as students they similarly become adept at knowing their teacher's view of where the normal limits of appropriate behavior are. Those who are slow at picking up such signals generally experience a lot of grief with their teacher.

It is important that students learn that the dividing line between what is appropriate and inappropriate is subjective, but it can still require compliance. Traffic laws provide many good illustrations. For example, the law cannot argue that it is logically better to drive on either the right or the left side of the street, but it can logically insist that everyone going the same direction must drive on the same side. If we have stopped at a stoplight, and absolutely no traffic is coming from any direction, should we wait for the green signal? Is it all right for a pedestrian at a *wait* signal to *walk* if no cars are in sight? Is it inappropriate for a driver going straight to pull up to a stoplight in the right lane and so prevent drivers behind him from making a right turn during the red light? We confront situations like these all the time.

Humor and the arts are perhaps so culturally pervasive because they both help us constantly explore the dividing line between appropriate and inappropriate behavior in pretend rather than in real-life situations (such as with the traffic signal problems above). We especially need to constantly explore the subtle shifts and discrepancies that move behaviors beyond the dividing line.

Our right frontal lobe contains modules that apparently process discrepancies (especially in linguistic information) and then pass such information on to our emotional thermostat, and this leads to responses (such as laughter and anger) that signal our assessment of the appropriateness of the situation. Because the frontal lobes of young children are not mature, they generally respond best to (and laugh at) broad discrepancies, such as in slapstick humor, rather than at subtle puns and other forms of word play that adults with mature frontal lobes enjoy. Young children can thus recognize very inappropriate behavior, but they often find it difficult to make fine discriminations and therefore to make appropriate judgments of their own behavior.

Students generally include "a sense of humor" when asked to identify preferred teacher characteristics. This suggests that students (perhaps unconsciously) appreciate teachers who can recognize student behavior that is getting close to or is right over the line and respond (at least initially) with a communicative smile or wink rather than a premature expression of anger. Insert this understanding of humor into your explorations of classroom management. Seeing the inappropriateness to absurdity of a situation with an expression that signals humor can defuse a tense classroom confrontation of what or who is right.

The comedian Stephen Wright is known for his absurd but subtle jokes, many of which revolve around a play on a single word: "I got interested in astronomy, and so I installed a skylight. The people in the apartment above me are furious"; "If the cops arrest a mime, do they have to tell him he has the right to remain silent?" The subtle turn on the words *apartment* and *mime* are key to getting the humor in the jokes, and both require a somewhat sophisticated understanding of the inappropriate behavioral absurdities described. Only an educator would truly appreciate the comment a teacher once made to me that she wanted to die during an inservice workshop because the transition from life to death would be so subtle.

The arts similarly are a marvelous vehicle for exploring what is appropriate and inappropriate because the arts do not try to solve problems with a simple true/false solution. Rather, they use pretend situations that are removed from reality to explore right and wrong. The arts do not merely depict something, they metaphorically analyze it in a way that forces folks to find an equivalent issue in their own life. So as you use the arts (and humor) in helping students understand issues in classroom management, help them get as close they can to the subtleties in the discrepancies that define the issue they are trying to understand and resolve.

In the End

Appropriate behavior is a two-sided coin. What do students have a right to expect from educators? What do educators have a right to expect from students?

Reasonable Student Expectations. Chapter 1 began with Dewey's strong belief that democratic values must permeate schools that hope to educate citizens capable of functioning effectively in a democratic society. These would include (a) constitutional rights to free speech, privacy, and due process; (b) legal rights to a quality education in a safe, nonrestrictive, nonharassing environment; and (c) a policy of distributed participation in decision making such as with classroom management issues and procedures. The courts have generally given schools some slack when educators unilaterally prohibit controversial behaviors they believe will reduce educational effectiveness, but it is not a good idea to lean on the constitutional and the fundamental human rights of students in doing it. Even if a school wins in court, it tends to lose support in the community and often ends up the focus of ridicule.

Students also have a right to expect that educators will operate with the dignity and integrity of adult behavior but at a personally pleasant level that is appropriate to someone who is working with immature students. Students further have a right to teachers who understand the curriculum and have mastered basic instructional and management skills. We can probably reduce it all down to an expectation that teachers should be interesting, curious, and fair adults. The old adage is that the quantity of student misbehavior is directly related to the quality of the teacher's behavior. Well, okay, plus a lot of other things that teachers cannot control. The reality is, though, that the only thing we can really control is the quality of our own classroom behavior and instruction, and we ought to take care of our part of the equation despite what others might do.

Teachers who constantly complain about all the things that students cannot and will not do are like custodians who complain about dirty floors. Dirty floors help define their job. Similarly, the considerable inabilities of students define a teacher's job. If you do not appreciate student ignorance, eradicate it!

This book has strongly suggested that classroom management ought to be an important part of the curriculum. The classroom management curriculum best functions in an exploratory environment that enthusiastically involves students in the observation, study, and analysis of their own behavior (and its underlying biological substrate) and then encourages them to creatively explore new ways of solving practical classroom management problems. Proposed solutions do not always have to work (the problem that a class is trying to solve is an example of something that is not working). If a proposal does not work, try something else. It is the exploratory environment of shared management that is the important element. It is process, not product.

Reasonable School Expectations. What should educators expect of students? They are personally immature and will communicate it in many amazing ways. They come with a stunning array of immature cognitive systems and an innate drive to further develop them in or out of school, whoever makes the best offer. They truly want to develop friendships, but their immature social skills often thwart their best-laid plans. Their out-of-school family and community life strongly impacts their school life. They depend heavily on adults to support them, and so they are appropriately concerned when the support is weak or absent, and school work moves well down the priority list at such times. They grouse a lot about school and its expectations, but most (at least secretly) like to go to school because that is where their friends are.

Teachers have a right to expect that students will help maintain an environment that is conducive to learning and that they will work to learn the things that the community deems important. That is not an unreasonable expectation. Students are not currently productive citizens, but our society has a right to insist that they master the minimum knowledge and skills required of productive adults, whether they like it or not. We are a social species, so individuals do not have a right to expect that others will support them throughout their lifetime. Teachers have a right to be quite assertive about this.

The preceding paragraph is not an authoritarian dictum in a classroom in which students are encouraged to participate in solving their own management issues. Students will come to understand it for what it is: a clear delineation of tasks and responsibilities as well as a shared commitment to work together.

However we manage a classroom, it is almost impossible to objectively define the subjective concept of *culturally appropriate.* Culturally appropriate is something we constantly negotiate in our own life and in our interactions with others. We expect others to operate within our idea of a normal range—behavior that is comfortable, familiar—and yet most of us constantly explore life beyond our normal range to see how it is.

People who live in big cities vacation in rural areas, and vice versa. People climb mountains and take tour boats to the Antarctica but have no plans to settle there. The success of such magazines as *People* suggests that we have a voyeuristic tendency to look in on (and perhaps cluck our tongues) at the behavior of celebrities, people who are well-known for their well-knownness, as Andy Worhol once put it. We further peek in on television shows that exploit the personal problems of noncelebrities who will claw and fight on

nationwide television for 10 minutes of celebrity, and like the rau-
cous studio audience that loudly indicates who it believes acted
appropriately and inappropriately, we also make our own private
judgments. We read the advice columns, letters to the editor, film
reviews, and the editorial columnists and then privately determine
our own beliefs about what is appropriate and inappropriate. We
get involved with election campaigns and local issues and then privately vote our own opinion on appropriate and inappropriate. It is
difficult to think of a day when we adults do not get involved with
these kinds of decisions hundreds of times.

So what is the normal range, and where are the edges that lead
to abnormality? Over time, students discover their teacher's beliefs
about the point at which behavior is unacceptable, and they will
realize that on some days the acceptable range is narrower or
broader than on other days. But they will finally get a handle on the
fluctuating realities of their teacher's expectations, and then a substitute teacher will show up one morning, and the first thing the
class will have to do without the help of their regular teacher is to
discover all over again the point at which normal behavior becomes
abnormal.

References and
Supplementary Readings

Barkow, J., Cosmides, L., & Tooby, J. (1992). *The adapted mind: Evolutionary psychology and the generation of culture.* New York: Oxford University Press.

Blackmore, S. (1999). *The meme machine.* New York: Oxford University Press.

Bower, B. (1995). Criminal intellects: Researchers look at why lawbreakers often brandish low I.Q.'s. *Science News, 147,*(15), 232-239.

Brownlee, S. (1997, February 17). Can't do without love: What science says about those tender feelings. *U.S. News and World Report,* pp. 58-60.

Butterworth, B. (1999). *What counts: How every brain is hardwired for math.* New York: Free Press.

Calvin, W. (1996a). *The cerebral code: Thinking a thought in the mosaics of the mind.* Cambridge, MA: MIT Press.

Calvin, W. (1996b). *How brains think. Evolving intelligence: Then and now.* New York: Basic Books.

Carter, R. (1998). *Mapping the mind.* Berkeley: University of California Press.

Clark, A. (1998). *Being there: Putting brain, body, and the world together again.* Cambridge, MA: MIT Press.

Coccaro, E. (1995, January). Biology of aggression. *Scientific American Science and Medicine,* pp. 38-47.

Damasio, A. (1999). *The feeling of what happens: Body and emotion in the making of consciousness*. New York: Harcourt Brace.

Davis, J. (1997). *Mapping the mind: The secrets of the human brain and how it works*. Secaucus, NJ: Birch Lane Press.

Dawkins, R. (1989a). *The selfish gene*. New York: Oxford University Press.

Dawkins, R. (1989b). *A river out of Eden: A Darwinian view of life*. New York: Basic Books.

Dehaene, S. (1997). *The number sense: How the mind creates mathematics*. New York: Oxford University Press.

DeWaal, F. (1996). *Good natured: The origins of right and wrong in humans and other animals*. Cambridge, MA: Harvard University Press.

Dewey, J. (1938). *Experience and education*. New York: Macmillan.

Diamond, M., & Hopson, J. (1998). *The magic trees of the mind: How to nurture your child's intelligence, creativity, and healthy emotions from birth through adolescence*. New York: Dutton.

DiGiulio, R. (1995). *Positive classroom management: A step-by-step guide to successfully running the show without destroying student dignity*. Thousand Oaks, CA: Corwin.

Dozier, R. (1998). *Fear itself: The origin and nature of the powerful emotion that shapes our lives and our world*. New York: St. Martin's.

Edelman, G. (1992). *Bright air, brilliant fire: On the matter of the mind*. New York: Basic Books.

Elbert, T., Pantex, C., Weinbruch, C., Rockstroh, B., & Taub, E. (1995). Increased cortical representations on the fingers of the left hand in string players. *Science, 270*, 305-306.

Fast For Word. (1997). Berkeley, CA: Scientific Learning Corporation.

Fuller. R. (1995, July). Neural functions of serotonin. *Scientific American Science and Medicine*, pp. 48-52.

Gardner, H. (1983). *Frames of mind: The theory of multiple intelligences*. New York: Basic Books.

Gardner, H. (1998). A multiplicity of intelligences. *Scientific American Presents, 9*(4), 18-23.

Gevins, A. (1997). What to do with your own personal brain scanner. In R. Solso (Ed.), *Mind and brain sciences in the 21st century* (pp. 111-126). Cambridge, MA: MIT Press.

Goleman, D. (1995). *Emotional intelligence: Why it can matter more than I.Q.* New York: Bantam.

Gootman, M. (1997). *The caring teacher's guide to discipline: Helping your students learn self-control, responsibility, and respect.* Thousand Oaks, CA: Corwin.

Hobson, J. (1994). *The chemistry of conscious states: How the brain changes its mind.* Boston: Little, Brown.

Holmes, T., & Rahe, R. (1967). The social readjustment rating scale. *Journal of Psychosomatic Research, 11,* 213-218.

Johns, T. (1990). *With bitter herbs they shall eat it: Chemical ecology and the origins of human diet and medicine.* Tucson: University of Arizona Press.

Johnson, D., & Johnson, R. (1995). *Reducing school violence through conflict resolution.* Alexandria, VA: Association for Supervision and Curriculum Development.

Kagan, J. (1994). *Galen's prophecy: Temperament in human nature.* New York: Basic Books.

Kandel, M., & Kandel, E. (1994). Flights of memory. *Discover Magazine, 15*(6), 32-38.

Kays, D. (1990). *A comparison of the attendance rates and patterns of fourth and fifth grade at-risk students in 27 elementary schools.* Unpublished doctoral dissertation, University of Oregon, Eugene.

Klawans, H. (1996). *Why Michael can't hit: And other tales of the neurology of sports.* New York: Freeman.

LeDoux, J. (1996). *The emotional brain: The mysterious underpinnings of emotional life.* New York: Simon & Schuster.

Lyons, M. (1977). *An inquiry into sixth grader pupils' responses to in-class waiting.* Unpublished doctoral dissertation, University of Oregon, Eugene.

Nesse, R., & Williams, G. (1994). *Why we get sick: The new science of Darwinian medicine.* New York: Random House.

Niehoff, D. (1999). *The biology of violence.* New York: Free Press.

Parasuraman, R. (1998). *The attentive brain.* Cambridge, MA: MIT Press.

Perkins, D. (1995). *Outsmarting I.Q.: The emerging science of learnable intelligence.* New York: Free Press.

Pert, C. (1997). *The molecules of emotion: Why you feel the way you feel.* New York: Scribner.

Pinker, S. (1997). *How minds work.* New York: Norton.

Posner, M., & Raichle, M. (1994). *Images of mind.* New York: Freeman.

Profet, M. (1992). Pregnancy sickness as adaptation: A deterrent to maternal ingestion of teratogens. In J. H. Barkow (Ed.), *The adapted mind* (pp. 327-365). New York: Oxford University Press.

Ridley, M. (1996). *The origins of virtue: Human instincts and the evolution of cooperation.* New York: Viking.

Rose, S. (1997). *Lifelines: Biology beyond determinism.* New York: Oxford University Press.

Rousell, L. (1992). *A comprehensive examination of grief themes in young children's books.* Unpublished doctoral dissertation, University of Oregon, Eugene.

Rymer, R. (1993). *Genie: An abused child's flight from silence.* New York: HarperCollins.

Sapolsky, R. (1997). Testosterone rules. *Discover Magazine, 18,* 45-50.

Sapolsky, R. (1998). *Why zebras don't get ulcers: An updated guide to stress, stress-related diseases, and coping.* New York: Freeman.

Sapolsky, R. (1999). Stress and your shrinking brain. *Discover Magazine, 20,* 116-122.

Short, P. R., & Blanton, C. (1994). *Rethinking student discipline: Alternatives that work.* Thousand Oaks, CA: Corwin.

Siegal, D. (1999). *The developing mind: Towards a neurobiology of interpersonal experience.* New York: Guilford.

Sternberg, R. (1985). *Beyond I.Q.: A triarchic theory of human intelligence.* New York: Cambridge University Press.

Sylwester, R. (1997a). Bioelectronic learning: The effects of electronic media on a developing brain. *Technos Quarterly, 6*(2), 19-23.

Sylwester, R. (1997b). The neurobiology of self-esteem and aggression. *Educational Leadership, 54*(5), 75-79.

Sylwester, R. (1998a). Art for the brain's sake. *Educational Leadership, 56*(3), 31-35.

Sylwester, R. (1998b). The brain revolution. *The School Administrator, 55*(1), 6-8.

Sylwester, R. (Ed.). (1998c). *Student brains, school issues: A collection of articles.* Arlington Heights, IL: Skylight.

Sylwester, R. (1999). In search of the roots of adolescent aggression. *Educational Leadership, 57*(1), 65-69.

Sylwester, R., & Margulies, N. (1998). *Discover your brain.* Tucson, AZ: Zephyr Press.

Volavka, J. (1995). *The neurobiology of violence.* Washington, DC: American Psychiatric Press.

Walker, H. (1998). First step to prevent antisocial behavior. *Teaching Exceptional Children, 30*(4), 16-19.

Walker, H., & Sylwester, R. (1998). Reducing students' refusal and resistance. *Teaching Exceptional Children, 30*(6), 52-57.

Werner, E., & Smith, R. (1992). *Overcoming the odds: High risk children from birth to adulthood.* Ithaca, NY: Cornell University Press.

Wilson, E. O. (1998). *Consilience: The unity of knowledge.* New York: Knopf.

Wright, R. (1994). *The moral animal: Why we are the way we are: The new science of evolutionary psychology.* New York: Pantheon.

Wright, R. (1995, March 13). The biology of violence. *The New Yorker,* pp. 66-77.

Wurtman, J., & Suffes, S. (1996). *The serotonin solution: The potent brain chemical that can help you to stop bingeing, lose weight, and feel great.* New York: Fawcett Columbine.

Index

Date Due

IF YOUR BOOK IS RECALLED YOUR DUE DATE WILL BE SHORTENED. YOU WILL BE NOTIFIED BY MAIL.